Praise for *Only Dead on the Inside*

"The quintessential guide on the topic. It will make you laugh; it will make you think; it will make you wonder the barter value of your children in case things get crazy. You need this book if you wanna live."

—Kevin Sussman, actor on the hit CBS sitcom *The Big Bang Theory*

"I have to admit: I giggled."

—Jessica Lahey, *New York Times* bestselling author of *The Gift of Failure*

"At first I was like, 'Oh, great, another hilarious parenting book written by a viral internet sensation. Just what the world doesn't need.' But then I finally read *Only Dead on the Inside* and realized this was a hilarious parenting book by a viral internet sensation *with zombies* and I was like, 'I was wrong. The world does need this!' You'll chortle, you'll chuckle, and you might even learn something."

—Jen Mann, *New York Times* bestselling author of *People I Want to Punch in the Throat: Competitive Crafters, Drop-Off Despots, and Other Suburban Scourges*

"This guide to parenting through the apocalypse is so darkly hilarious, you don't even need to be a parent or have experienced an apocalypse to enjoy it."

—Liz Climo, artist for *The Simpsons*, author, and creator of viral comics on lizclimo.tumblr.com

"Are you a parent of cute, selfish, tiny people who look like you but don't pay rent, destroy your sleep, inspire homicidal thoughts, and shatter your self-confidence daily? Do you need help to survive this crisis? (Yes, yes you do.) Long-suffering parent, you must immediately read James Breakwell's hilarious, fast-paced, and practical book chock-full of wisdom, to-do lists, rules, and big pie charts and graphs. Breakwell not only taught me how

to survive the madness of parenthood, but also how to protect my babies from becoming undead, crawling, brain-eating monsters in diapers after the inevitable zombie apocalypse."

—Wajahat Ali, speaker and *New York Times* op-ed contributor

"This book is hilarious! I couldn't put it down (out of fear for my life and that of future generations). This guide is the ultimate weapon against fighting zombies, which is the scariest prospect second only to parenting. I would put this novel in the self-help section with a seal of Oprah's approval, because not only does it help you live your best life, it finally gives you a good reason for owning that cumbersome stroller."

—Abbi Crutchfield, stand-up comedian and host of *You Can Do Better* on truTV

"The case is made for why parents will be the ultimate survivors of the Zombie Apocalypse. Whether it's using the 'unreliability of your children to your advantage' or benefitting from the enmity a normal game of Monopoly can conjure, Breakwell pulls everyday scenarios for parents and hilariously weaponizes them for your survival. Plus, any book that uses the phrase 'catastrophic bowel movements' is a book I want to read."

—Patrick Quinn, cofounder of Life of Dad, a social network for fathers

"I never laugh out loud and this book is so funny I stopped reading to drag my family members in to read paragraphs to them but I'd do a terrible job of reading because I kept giggling about what I was reading. It's kind of about zombies, more about parenting, but mostly a reason to write one hilarious sentence after the next. James Breakwell is so good at being funny that it kind of makes me angry, but then I'd read another page and laugh like an idiot again. You need this book."

—Quinn Cummings, author of *Notes from the Underwire* and *The Year of Learning Dangerously*

"James Breakwell is the Dr. Spock of the apocalypse and his no-nonsense guide to raising happy, healthy kids as the world spirals into blood-soaked chaos and unspeakable brain-eating horror belongs in every home. When the undead come knocking, you'll burn all your other parenting books for fuel. Breakwell gives you the real-world, end-of-world strategies that you simply won't find anywhere else. Your family will survive and even thrive in the zombie apocalypse while parents who bought guides to raising gifted kids go down in the first wave. Wouldn't you rather have this book and not need it, than need it not have it?"

—Eileen Curtright, author of *The Burned Bridges of Ward, Nebraska*

"If the only line in this book was, 'The fat shall inherit the earth,' I would still urgently recommend this book because it will have validated my entire existence. But even if you are a naturally skinny asshole whose thighs have never touched, you need this book. Because for once, your time will not be wasted worrying about fake threats like Putin and ISIS, but the very real threat of the undead coming to suck on your scrawny bones. Which doesn't sound so terrible if you're exhausted from raising the living parasites you birthed, but trust me, this isn't about you. It's not even about your thankless progeny. It's about saving the little bloodsuckers that call you Mom and Dad from being bitten by zombies in order to ensure the future of the human race. Which is a debatable end goal, too, so strike that. Read this book because it will make you giggle uncontrollably, cry like no one's watching, and wonder if becoming a zombie isn't so bad after all. Eighteen stars. Highly recommended."

—Rabia Chaudry, attorney and *New York Times* bestselling author of *Adnan's Story: The Search for Truth and Justice After* Serial

ONLY DEAD

ON THE INSIDE

ONLY DEAD
ON THE INSIDE

A PARENT'S GUIDE TO SURVIVING
THE ZOMBIE APOCALYPSE

JAMES
BREAKWELL

BenBella Books, Inc.
Dallas, TX

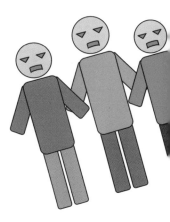

BenBella

BenBella Books, Inc.
10440 N. Central Expressway, Suite 800
Dallas, TX 75231
www.benbellabooks.com
Send feedback to feedback@benbellabooks.com

Printed in the United States of America
10 9 8 7 6 5 4 3 2 1

Library of Congress Cataloging-in-Publication Data
Names: Breakwell, James, author.
Title: Only dead on the inside : a parent's guide to the zombie apocalypse / James Breakwel.
Description: Dallas, TX : BenBella Books, Inc., [2017] | Includes bibliographical references and index.
Identifiers: LCCN 2017008274 (print) | LCCN 2017025322 (ebook) | ISBN 9781944648640 (electronic) | ISBN 9781944648633 (trade paper : alk. paper)
Subjects: LCSH: Zombies—Humor. | Parenting—Humor.
Classification: LCC PN6231.Z65 (ebook) | LCC PN6231.Z65 B73 2017 (print) | DDC 818/.602—dc23
LC record available at https://lccn.loc.gov/2017008274

Editing by Leah Wilson
Copyediting by James Fraleigh
Proofreading by Kimberly Broderick and Rachel Phares
Text design and composition by Aaron Edmiston
Front cover design by Ty Nowicki
Full cover design by Ivy Koval
Author photograph by David Van Deman
Printed by Versa Press

Distributed by Perseus Distribution
www.perseusdistribution.com

To place orders through Perseus Distribution:
Tel: (800) 343-4499
Fax: (800) 351-5073
E-mail: orderentry@perseusbooks.com

Special discounts for bulk sales (minimum of 25 copies) are available.
Please contact Aida Herrera at aida@benbellabooks.com.

To my wife and kids, for letting me tell the truth.
And countless lies.

To everyone who ever read my jokes on the internet,
this is all your fault.

CONTENTS

WELCOME TO THE END

If you're reading this, congratulations: You're still alive. Only uninfected humans can read. Illiteracy is one of the worst side effects of zombieism, second only to the insatiable hunger for human flesh. In those places where school is still in session, the undead will have a devastating effect on standardized test scores. If you're a zombie, you're no doubt looking at this page with confused disinterest. Perhaps you'll bite it in the fleeting hope it might be edible, only to be disappointed. If it makes you feel better, people who read it will have the same reaction. Letting people down is what I do best. I'm a dad.

It's not easy being a parent these days. There are bills to pay, children to feed, and hordes of undead monsters to keep at bay. How a person juggles these duties separates a good provider from a dead one. Make no mistake: The zombie apocalypse is real. If it hasn't reached you yet, it's on its way as surely as autumn follows summer or regret follows vodka. As the unstoppable masses of undead march forward, national governments will crumble and local leaders will flee. Only the basic family unit will survive. In the anarchy of the post-apocalyptic world, parents will be the highest-ranking authority figures by default. That thought is more terrifying than any walking corpse. Once the zombie apocalypse begins in earnest, the fate of the world will rest on your spit-up–covered shoulders. Now is a good time to panic.

That's why this book matters. There are lots of guides out there about how to survive when the dead walk the earth. All of them assume readers are young, fit, and unencumbered by miniature versions of themselves. According to that scenario, the only humans left will be smug, outdoorsy Millennials. Even without the zombies, that's the textbook definition of hell on earth.

But contrary to what Generation Y will tell you, children are kind of important. Without them, the human race will go extinct. *Homo sapiens* have passed their genes from one generation to the next through eons of ice ages, plagues, and wars. It seems ungrateful to throw in the towel now because of one measly zombie apocalypse.

For the human race to survive, children must survive. And for them to make it, moms and dads have to up their game.

They don't have to be the best parents in the world. They just have to be slightly less crappy parents than normal. Quite frankly, that still might be asking too much. Even in the best of times, most of us barely get by. Modern moms and dads wear many hats, mostly to hide our stress-induced hair loss. Parents are breadwinners, chauffeurs, maintenance workers, playmates, enforcers, and coaches. Throw in a worldwide epidemic that makes people eat each other, and there's very little chance anyone will make it to soccer practice on time. None of these jobs will get easier after the world ends—except maybe coaching. A win is a win, even when the other team forfeits because it was eaten by zombies.

TAG-TEAMING THE APOCALYPSE

Raising children is a two-parent job, and that's doubly true in the zombie apocalypse. Unfortunately, most children don't have four parents. Kids will have to get by with however many guardians they have left, which will usually be somewhere between zero and two. I'm not here to judge which type of living arrangement is best for kids. That leads to drama, which is noisy and gets people eaten. I try to keep casualties to a minimum.

It's hard to define a modern family even when the dead aren't walking the earth. For the purposes of this guide, a family is any group of individuals who band together to keep children alive. That can include any combination of moms, dads, stepparents, grandparents, sketchy people met on the road, wolves that find and raise babies, balls with bloody handprints on them, and talking smartphone interfaces. I envy anyone who gets to co-parent with Siri.

This diversity makes it impossible to address every type of family without leaving someone out. I don't have time to rewrite every paragraph sixteen different ways to point out how a family with two dads might handle a situation differently than a family with a single mom and a volleyball. Unless my publisher decides to pay me by the word, in which case I'll do exactly that. You'll know I went that route if this book is twice as thick as the Bible.

But if this book is a reasonable thickness, I kept things simple and addressed my advice toward a family with one mom and one dad. If that doesn't describe your household, swap the pronouns or number of parents in your head and it'll still work. Or pay someone to go through the book with a marker and change it for you. There are a lot of starving editors on the streets. Help a few of them feed their children tonight.

REALITY CHECK

The old challenges of everyday life will vanish the instant zombies show up—but not one second sooner. That's one of the biggest obstacles parents face that other survival guides overlook: Ordinary life will continue until the moment it ends for good. There won't be a transition period when moms and dads can quit their jobs, cash out their kids' college funds, and spend six months digging a bunker out in the desert. There will be bills to pay right up to the second civilization collapses and money loses all value forever. Then millions of greenbacks won't be worth as much as a single serving of beans. That's why you should toss a few extra cans in your cart every time you go to the grocery store. Someday you'll be the richest person in the world.

Until that time, however, vigilant parents will face skeptics who think preparing for the zombie apocalypse is wasteful at best and dangerous at worst. Don't worry. Those naysayers will die in the first wave. There's no sweeter revenge than natural selection.

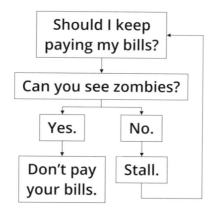

There's another reason why, as a parent, you can't drop everything to get ready for zombies, no matter how sure you are that the end is near. You must maintain a semblance of normality to avoid scaring your children and destroying your marriage. While there are occasional exceptions, at least one spouse in every relationship is firmly against dipping into the family budget to pursue the paranoid delusions of a selfish man-child. That last part may or may not be a direct quote from my wife. When I slipped on that wedding ring, I got more than a partner for life; I gained a standing veto to all my best schemes. Marriage has a built-in system of checks and balances. The checks aren't so much like Congress checking a president as they are like one hockey player checking another into a wall. It hurts, but it's also a wakeup call—assuming you ever wake up.

HOW THIS BOOK WORKS

This book guides parents through the unique child-rearing challenges of the zombie apocalypse. If you don't believe in zombies, you might still find this book entertaining. It'll help you pass the time until the undead eat you. Before you die, you might even pick up a tip or two on how to raise children when zombies aren't around. That's not my goal. Any normal parenting lessons you learn from this book are strictly accidental.

This guide uses several methods to teach parents about surviving the zombie apocalypse:

WORDS

In a novel approach no one ever thought of before, I converted thoughts from my head into strings of text on paper. By reading those words, you'll download my ideas directly into your mind. I arrayed these brain codes as horizontal lines throughout this book. Read them left to right, moving down a line after completing each one. Blink as necessary. Don't worry if my thoughts give you a headache. That happens all the time to my wife.

COMICS

These three-panel stories illustrate lessons about raising kids around zombies. Sometimes, they pertain directly to the text of this book. Other times, well, they don't. Give me a break. I had a lot of blank space to fill.

The art style of these comics is deliberately Spartan. Beautiful, detailed images would be too distracting. I don't want your eyes to linger on a stunning, emotionally complex image when a zombie could sneak up behind you at any moment. Also, I suck at drawing and this is legitimately the best I could do. I can't believe people paid money for this book.

GRAPHS

Numbers are scary. Math might not bite you and turn you into an undead monster, but it can ruin your chances of getting into medical school and turn you into a struggling humor writer for the rest of your life. Not that I'm bitter or anything. To make the data in this book more user-friendly, I broke it down into colorful charts and graphs. Each one offers in-depth statistical information I made up off the top of my head. But every bit of it is true because it's published right here. You can't lie in a book. I think it's illegal.

DO'S AND DON'TS

Despite being a straightforward concept, a zombie survival guide for parents is still a hard idea for some people to wrap their heads around. Just ask the dozens and dozens of people who gave me blank stares when I pitched this book. My ideas are the world's leading cause of awkward silences.

To help everyone who still doesn't get where I'm going with this, I've made a list of dos and don'ts to walk you through it. That's right: There's a guide for this zombie guide. If you fail to understand that, there is no guide for the guide for the guide. You'll have to wing it.

✓ **Do** reference this book when you need quick, concise information on how to survive a specific zombie situation.

✗ **Don't** read this book while being actively attacked by zombies. No book is worth dying for. Except the one that came down to us from a higher power. I'm talking, of course, about *Harry Potter and the Deathly Hallows*. J. K. Rowling be with you.

✓ **Do** use this book to hit zombies, but only if there are no better weapons available AND you bought the special metal-plated edition. If you have the paperback, you're out of luck.

✗ **Don't** eat this book. Food is scarce in the zombie apocalypse, but this published work has little nutritional value. Also, it might hurt when it comes back out, especially if you're reading this on a tablet.

✓ **Do** get a copy of this book you can keep. If you use it right, it'll be covered in dirt and blood splatter by the end. The last thing you need in the apocalypse is a hefty library fine.

✗ **Don't** tell your friends about this book. You need every advantage you can get over the competition. It's a person-eat-person world out there.

✓ **Do** take this book literally. It's about raising kids in the zombie apocalypse. Everything in here is obviously true. If there's parenting advice you don't like, get offended. Write an angry letter.

If possible, light something on fire. That's the only appropriate response to this very real threat to your parenting style. I don't even know what sarcasm is. A zombie ate my dictionary.

FINAL WAIVER

It's possible for you and your entire family to make it through the zombie apocalypse alive and well if you do precisely what I tell you. I'm perhaps the most qualified man on the planet to teach these lessons. I have four daughters, and as of today not a single one of them has died in a zombie attack. No one alive has faced more zombies than I have. Then again, no one has faced less. We're all tied at zero.

Nonetheless, I stand behind my words. If you read this book, I guarantee you won't die in a zombie attack. I'm not sure how you'll collect the money if I'm wrong, but that's not my problem. This isn't a step-by-step guide for how zombies can sue unscrupulous authors. But with any luck, it won't come to that.

Just as a journey of a thousand miles begins with a single step, a book of twelve chapters begins with one excessively wordy introduction. It's going to be a wild ride. Buckle up, but only metaphorically. You shouldn't ever read this book in a moving vehicle. You need to keep both eyes on the road to watch for zombies.

CHAPTER 1

THE BEST BAD DAY OF YOUR LIFE

You can't pick when and where zombies will attack. Even if you tried, the undead are notoriously bad at keeping appointments. That's why you should be prepared at all times to fight for your life. This readiness should start well before civilization collapses. It's easy to be on guard when the dead are already walking the earth, but it takes much more discipline to be vigilant when the biggest dangers in your life are being late for a PTA meeting or burning a frozen pizza. For the record, the instructions were not as clear as they could have been, and the smoke damage was minimal. Remind me to send a gift basket to the fire department.

The zombie apocalypse won't start everywhere at once. In some areas, it could be underway right now. It's easy to mistake an undead assault for something else, like "civil unrest" or "boy band concerts." In other areas, zombie attacks could take months or even years to begin. Portland will be ground zero for the outbreak. People there do everything before it's cool. San Francisco will be the last to fall. The undead can't afford the rent, even for homes damaged by unexplained pizza fires.

The zombie apocalypse won't start with fireworks and a laser light show. The undead are more understated than that, and besides, they don't have the budget. Instead, it'll be up to parents to look for subtle signs the dead are walking the earth. In some places, this will be easy to spot. In Canada, where the crime rate is zero and no one has said a swear word since 1982, even one zombie could throw the whole country into chaos. In other places, zombies could destroy everything and nobody would notice the difference. I'm looking at you, New Jersey.

As a parent, it's crucial that you time your response exactly right. If you quit your job and pull your kids out of school too early, you'll starve to death before the zombie apocalypse even starts. But if you wait too long, everyone you love could be eaten by zombies, which would make for an awkward family newsletter. Making the right decision requires maturity, vision, and excellent judgment. Too bad it's up to you.

There are simple steps you can take every day to ensure you catch the end of the world right at the start. The first thing you should do when you wake up is look out the window. As a kid, I checked if there was enough snow to cancel school; now I check if there are enough zombies to cancel work. Most days, I'm disappointed. Never get your hopes up when it comes to Mother Nature or the damned.

Remember to always do a visual check. Zombies, like weather, are local. Just because the entire region is expecting a big storm doesn't mean your house will get a drop of rain. In the same way, just because nobody else has seen a zombie yet doesn't mean the very first one isn't lurking in your bushes. Cut down all hedges as a precaution. At the very least, you won't have to trim them every year.

Next, check the news. That term is misleading. As anyone who has ever watched or read it knows, there's very little news in the news. If important stories get covered, it's strictly by accident. Reporters are mainly interested in celebrities, sex scandals, and sensational crimes. Sure, they might mention a politician every now and then, but only if they're involved in the sexy murder of someone famous. Even the most obscure legislator can make international headlines if his mistress dies in a sex swing accident at a petting zoo. That's how "sexident" and "zooscrew" made their way into the dictionary.

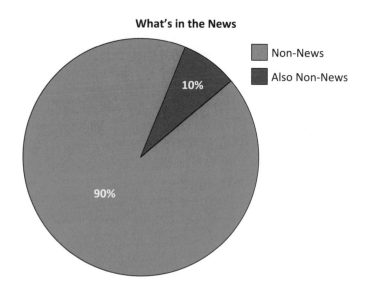

What's in the News

Non-News

Also Non-News

10%

90%

Carefully screen any news story that sounds vaguely zombie-related. There are a lot of false positives. Stampedes and mass groups of panicked people killing each other aren't proof of anything. Look at any Black Friday sale. If you won't bite off someone's ear to get a discounted TV, you don't deserve it. The same goes for riots. Chaos in the streets proves the existence of a local sports team, not zombies. Nothing shows civic pride quite like torching your own city.

IF IT'S ALL CLEAR

If there are no zombies outside your window or in the news, prepare for the worst: real life. The most awful moment on any morning is when you realize the world isn't going to end and you have to go to work. Until humanity reverts to a post-apocalyptic barter economy, you have to earn a paycheck. I look forward to the day when I can pay for my daughters' braces with a bag of pinecones.

The area might be zombie-free when you walk out the front door, but that doesn't mean it'll stay that way all day. A good parent needs to be ready for all hell to break loose at a moment's notice. Undead swarms seldom call ahead. My wife and I both work, and it's my job to drop off the kids at school and daycare. Parents still have a duty to protect their partners and children, even if they have to do it from a distance. If my family gets eaten, I won't get another one. I beat the odds when I found one woman willing to reproduce with me. I will never, ever be that lucky again. Most other dads find themselves in the same situation. In a way, families with bumbling losers for fathers are the fortunate ones. Our wives and kids know we have to protect them because we don't have a plan B.

To keep your children safe, carefully vet their daycare provider. This means daily, not just once a year before you pay your deposit. Shockingly, many parents refuse to take an extra five minutes before dropping their kids off to verify their daycare isn't overrun by zombies. Children in that age range are unlikely to defend themselves effectively against the undead. For unknown reasons, the government discourages firearms training for toddlers.

The chances of a zombie outbreak beginning in a daycare are alarmingly high. Toddlers are walking Petri dishes. Every major illness starts with them. They are so contagious that NATO's current germ warfare policy is to parachute preschoolers into enemy countries. A single runny nose could wipe out North Korea. Little kids have undeveloped immune systems and love to eat food off the floor. To diseases, they're Disneyland. Put twelve toddlers in a room together and you'll have the deadliest germ laboratory in the world. Everyone knows the bubonic plague started in a daycare. I don't see why the first case of zombieism will be any different.

Daycares may be child death traps, but they're also convenient. The only alternative is to have one parent stay home with the kids, and that's a sacrifice most families won't make. Love is good, but disposable income is better. The best compromise is to minimize the risks at daycare as much as possible while still working full time. Every day when you drop off your kids, ask four lifesaving questions:

1. Does the teacher have any obvious bite marks?
2. Is the play space covered in dismembered body parts?
3. Are the children trying to satisfy their unending hunger for human flesh?
4. Is anything on fire?

If the answer to even one of these questions is "yes," keep your kids home that day—unless you've already paid for the whole week. Then leave your kids there, because money doesn't grow on trees. There's no point in asking for your check back. Zombies don't give refunds.

The same plan works for school-aged children. Unlike daycare, school is mandated by law. You'll need a very good reason to keep your kids home. Ongoing zombie attacks qualify, but only with a doctor's note. Always know what classrooms your kid will be in at which times of day in case you need to pull them out in a hurry. Make a special note of any skylights should you need to enter through the ceiling later. I have a grappling hook for just such an occasion. Unless my wife is reading this, in which case I'm joking. Please don't check the trunk.

Stay-at-home moms and dads can skip all these precautions and sit at home, smugly judging the rest of us. But there's a tradeoff for this haughty superiority. Stay-at-home parents don't answer to a big boss at a corporation, but they do answer to multiple tiny bosses in their own homes. There are no sick days from that job, and good luck quitting. It's against the law to give up on your children. So much for employee rights. I can't protect my family as well as a stay-at-home parent, but at least no matter how bad my day at work gets, I'll never have to change my boss's diaper.

The rest of us have to monitor our family members' safety from a distance. My kids don't have cell phones due to school rules and my own cheapness, but I text my wife throughout the day. I shoot her cute messages like "I love you" and "How are you feeling?" What I actually mean is "Are you still alive?" and "Should I leave work early to smash zombie skulls?" I can't say either of those things outright, though, because it always leads to a huge fight with lots of crying. I can't help it that I have overactive tear ducts. When I phrase my text messages more generically, my wife is more likely to reply. Once she messages me back, I know she hasn't been eaten or turned into a zombie. The undead don't text. It's their best quality.

ON-THE-JOB SAFETY

The safety of your family is important, but your own wellbeing matters, too. You can't protect anyone if you turn into a zombie—unless your family members tie you to the front of their car to use you as a meat shield. I don't recommend that unless you want to void the warranty.

Your mission is to stay alive at work, which isn't as easy as it sounds. At the start of the zombie apocalypse, the modern office is almost as dangerous as a daycare, just with fewer life-threatening diseases and more paper cuts.

As with escaping school and daycare, the key to getting out of work and back to your family is to make sure it's actually time to get out. Fleeing work because of zombies is a one-shot deal, so it has to be done right the first time. If you're a husband and you quit work when there's no danger, your wife will kill you. Literally. There's no way a story about resigning from your job for imaginary zombies doesn't end with spousal murder. The judge will let your wife off with a warning.

Here are a few scenarios to help you figure out when to take a personal day for the end of the world.

Scenario 1:

You hear screams from the other side of the room. A man fights for his life against a coworker who is on top of him. As they roll, they knock a stack of Styrofoam cups and an empty doughnut box off a table. Should you panic?

No. Somebody ate the last doughnut. Given the level of anger involved, they likely ate two or more and left someone else with none. What you see isn't a zombie attack; it's good old-fashioned vigilante justice.

Scenario 2:

Janice from accounting viciously mauls Stan, the guy who always shows you pictures of his cat. Stan appears to be dead. There's blood everywhere. Inexplicably, you're the only one who notices. Is this a zombie attack?

Maybe.

It's possible Stan simply showed Janice one feline snapshot too many. Everyone has a breaking point.

However, there's one sure sign this attack is real: Everyone else is ignoring it. When a situation is serious, your coworkers will pretend they hear nothing while eavesdropping as intensely as possible. If Janice and Stan were having a normal disagreement, everyone would stand up and gawk. But since one or more people could be fired—Janice for being a zombie and eating Stan, and Stan for bleeding everywhere and ruining company property—your colleagues look the other way.

Congratulations, this is a real zombie attack. This is great news for you since you get to leave work early. It's not such great news for Stan.

If you find a real zombie attack, take a moment to collect yourself. It's a big milestone. It means most of the people you know and love will die horrific deaths. It also means you'll never have to sit in a cubicle again. On the whole, it's a good day. One victory fist pump is acceptable, but two or more is bragging. Your dying coworker might find that a bit classless. Besides, you'll need your fist to fight off this zombie and any others on the premises.

SHOWTIME

Now is when the real fun begins. Retrieve your kids, rendezvous with your spouse, and settle in for the apocalypse. The whole experience is terrifying and exhilarating at the same time. It's exactly what you felt when you first became a parent.

CHAPTER 2

KAMIKAZE KIDS

In an ordinary survival guide, this is the point where the author would explain what a zombie is. To hell with that. You've seen them on TV. They're slow. They're stupid. You have to hit them in the head. I just saved you the fifteen dollars you would've wasted on someone else's zombie book. Feel free to mail me a kickback.

Rather than tell you what you already know, this chapter is about something that's a mystery to everyone: children. If you're going to risk your life to lead these tiny, ungrateful humanoids through the ruins of civilization, you'll need to understand what makes them tick. For starters, children don't actually tick. If yours does, consult a doctor.

Don't be fooled by grade inflation and participation trophies. Kids suck at everything. They're the worst zombie apocalypse teammates imaginable. Don't worry, it's not your fault. Except for the genes you gave them. And all the parenting you've done. But other than that, you're blameless.

Kids are selfish, short-sighted, and unreliable. All parents know this, but some still believe their offspring will come through for them in a crisis. That's the sort of naive optimism that gets people killed. The media loves stories about children who save their families from fires or floods, but these incidents are only newsworthy because they're rare. You're as likely to see a heroic child as you are to spot a chupacabra or a clean public restroom. To date, there's no conclusive proof of either one.

Outside of feel-good fluff pieces, children don't help anyone, not even themselves. They're worse than useless; they're suicidal. This is by design. Kids purposely disobey everything their parents tell them even though it's meant to keep them safe. No one is ordering these kids to hang out in abandoned mine shafts or shoot heroin. Instead, mothers and fathers say crazy things like "Eat your vegetables" and "Don't play in traffic." In return, their sons and daughters do their best to end up as nutritionally deprived roadkill. Luckily, they seldom succeed. Children even suck at dying.

BORN THIS WAY

After countless generations of this behavior, you'd think natural selection would favor children who follow the life-saving advice of their parents. The fact that modern kids are stubborn jerks proves otherwise. And contrary to popular belief, the most disagreeable children don't turn into the most intelligent adults. That's just something scientists tell parents to keep them from drinking themselves to death. The only difference between a research paper and a white lie is grant money.

Horrible children might not make sense individually, but they have a purpose if you look at them on a larger scale. Bad offspring prevent humans from overpopulating the earth. True, the world is already overcrowded, but the situation would be worse if families in developed countries each had eight kids rather than a manageable 2.2. Modern parents are richer, have better medical care, and live in a safer environment than parents in any other era of history. Now that the struggle for the survival of our species is over, mothers and fathers could pump out large families as a sort of victory lap. Our spoiled, entitled children ensure that will never happen. Doubt the link all you want, but the fact remains that when prosperity in a nation goes up, the birth rate goes down. As life gets better, our kids get worse. And they do it to save us all.

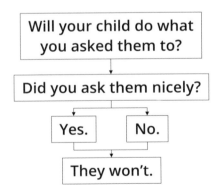

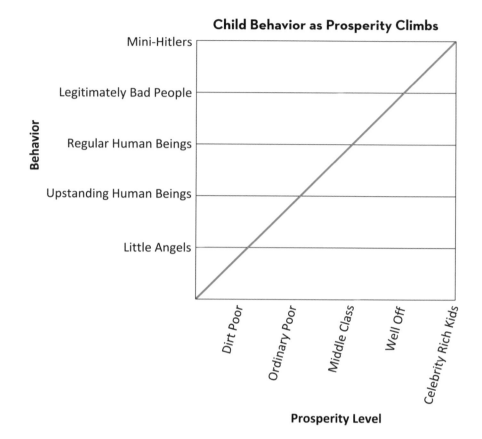

Child Behavior as Prosperity Climbs

y-axis (Behavior, bottom to top): Little Angels, Upstanding Human Beings, Regular Human Beings, Legitimately Bad People, Mini-Hitlers

x-axis (Prosperity Level, left to right): Dirt Poor, Ordinary Poor, Middle Class, Well Off, Celebrity Rich Kids

WARNING: CHILDREN AHEAD

The world isn't inherently dangerous, at least not before the zombies show up. Children simply go out of their way to die. Life is full of odd disclaimers caused by the inexplicable things kids of all ages do. Don't stick forks in electric outlets. Don't douse a paper bag full of fireworks in gasoline and light it on fire. Don't throw that bag in a pasture full of sleeping cows. Don't do all of these things in a row in one epic weekend and post the video on social media. Maybe the impending collapse of the internet isn't such a bad thing.

To adults, all that seems like common sense, but kids ranging in age from newborns to young adults need these reminders. Children are idiot savants at finding danger where there is none. Products designed specifically to keep minors alive are constantly being recalled because a few random kids somehow managed to kill themselves with them. It takes skill to make an inert wooden crib spontaneously burst into flames, but if anyone can do it, it's a six-month-old. Then the company that made the crib will get sued because it didn't anticipate the need for a baby sprinkler system. It's amazing the human race survived long enough to be wiped out by zombies.

Safety Devices That Inexplicably Kill Children

Device	Hidden Danger
Warning Label	Detaches and becomes a choking hazard.
Child Lock	Draws attention to the dangerous thing you're protecting. Takes kids seconds to break.
Safety Scissors	Just regular scissors with the word "safety" tacked on. Can still cut an artery during arts and crafts time.
Bike Helmet	Makes kids feel invincible. Leads to concussions and chronic headbutting.
Car Seat	Suffocates sleeping children. You must poke children every 30 seconds to keep them awake on long car rides.
Stuffed Animals	Teach kids that animals want to be cuddled. Lead to preschoolers jumping fences at zoo exhibits.
Baby Dolls	Teach kids that babies have hard, plastic heads and can be swung like a mace.

Only the prompt intervention of parents stops children's haphazard suicide attempts from succeeding. Moms and dads weren't always so effective. Back before modern medicine, parents had a much harder time protecting their kids from self-inflicted stupidity and child mortality rates were higher. Fatal mishaps weren't as big of a deal, though, because kids weren't viewed as unique and irreplaceable. Families were machines, and the children were interchangeable parts. There was no way to fix them, so if one broke, you swapped it out for a new one. Parents mass-produced children assuming almost none of them would survive to adulthood. Today, parents only have a few kids out of fear they all will.

Modern parents are right to dread their own living children. Caregivers innately understand that kids get worse as life gets better—even if no one is brave enough to admit it out loud. Officially, children are wonderful miracles in all circumstances, and anyone who says otherwise is a heartless troll. Rather than violate this taboo, parents fight back silently but decisively by having fewer children as the world improves. In that way, the population growth curve levels out. Eventually, society achieves an equilibrium where life is good and children are monstrous but scarce. It's an ideal situation—as long as you aren't a parent.

THE DEVIL YOU KNOW

All of this is important to remember once the zombie apocalypse arrives because the luxury and ease kids today are used to will suddenly vanish. The children you have to drag kicking and screaming through the end of the world will be the same ones who thought it was child abuse when you wouldn't buy them a new smartphone in middle school. They won't have an epiphany where they become cooperative and grateful to be alive. If they didn't thank you for raising them when your house was the nicest one in a great neighborhood, they definitely won't thank you when it has no electricity or running water and is surrounded by the damned.

The truth is kids understand the challenges parents face. They just don't care. Children have certain expectations, and they won't accept a lower standard of parenting simply because the dead are killing everyone. Young humans complain constantly even when the world revolves around them.

On a whininess scale of one to ten—with one being silence and ten being Caillou, an insufferable Canadian cartoon character created in a deliberate attempt to destroy America—most kids are normally around a three or a four. If civilization suddenly collapses and all its comforts disappear, that number will skyrocket to a figure calculable only by supercomputers or God. Infinity times ten sounds about right.

Anyone who thinks children will selflessly rise to the occasion has only read about kids in books. Real human children are narcissistic tyrants at best and slightly louder narcissistic tyrants at worst. Once the world ends, moms and dads will be tasked with keeping their tiny monsters alive in the face of adult-size monsters who want to eat them. In return, parents will be rewarded with an endless series of annoyed sighs and condescending eye rolls. Good luck.

The situation isn't entirely hopeless. Over time, the child behavior trend will reverse: As the world gets worse, successive generations of children will get better. Your children's children—if by some miracle your own sheltered offspring make it that long—will be born into a hard, uncaring world with few physical comforts. Nobody will give a damn about their self-esteem, and participation trophies will be as extinct as Wi-Fi and cable TV. A few generations later, your great-great-grandchildren will be like the hardscrabble pioneer kids of centuries ago who were happy if the only thing they got for their birthday was surviving dysentery. But you'll never meet those admirable descendants. You'll be long dead by then, hopefully in a hole in the ground but possibly as a zombie wandering the earth. It's too late for your own children, but it might be possible for your distant descendants to raise good kids. Let a more competent parent give it a try.

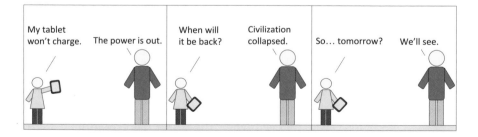

YOUR LOT IN LIFE

By now you understand that most generations of parents get either good children in bad times or bad children in good times. But present-day parents will have the unique distinction of raising bad children in bad times. It's your burden to protect bored, self-destructive kids as they plunge headlong into a world that actively tries to kill them. If they keep up their old ways, they'll be dead before the world's last pot of coffee gets cold. Hard times and caffeine shortages lie ahead. Enjoy that last cup.

The first step to prepare your kids is to make them understand the world has changed. The way you break the news will set the tone for the entire apocalypse. No pressure.

How to Tell Kids the World Ended

Age	Method
Baby	Make some cooing noises and maybe jingle some keys in their face. They'll get the message.
Toddler	"Remember how you were biting everybody? Well, it caught on."
Preschooler	"I can stay home and play with you today. There's no more work. There's no more anything."
Elementary School Student	"Everyone you've ever known or loved is dead. Pancakes?"
Junior High Student	"Puberty should be less awkward for you now that we're never going outside again."
High Schooler	"That college you wanted to get into should have a lot more openings."
Adult Children	"Time to move out."

EMOTIONAL APOCALYPSE

Your children will be devastated by the end of the world, but not for the reasons you think. The loss of human life won't faze them at all, but the fact they can't stream cartoons anymore will make them lose the will to live. Add this to children's already highly refined self-destructive tendencies and you'll be lucky if they don't spontaneously combust. It's your job to help them through this transition, not because they deserve your sympathy, but because without them the human race will cease to exist. They'll hold all the leverage in the zombie apocalypse. That much, at least, will stay the same.

Your children will go through all five stages of the grieving process. Since the cause of the zombie apocalypse is still a mystery, expect all blame to fall squarely on your shoulders. That's a familiar role. The only two qualifications to be a parent are to have a child and be a scapegoat.

It's possible that after the trauma of the apocalypse, your children will retract into themselves and withdraw from the world. They might even cut off all communication with others and enter a permanent sulk. If this happens, give your spouse a high-five. You hit the jackpot. Enjoy weeks, months, or even years of blissful quiet. Don't try to bring them out of their funk until they're close to adulthood. Then rouse them just enough to turn them into functional human beings and kick them out the door. It's the perfect system. Emotional trauma for the win.

A CLEAR VIEW

As long as you're honest about who your kids are and how they'll react to zombies, you should be fine. Actually, that's not true at all. There are hundreds of pages of other things you'll have to do to stay alive. But lowering your expectations for your kids is an important first step. As long as you count on them being absolutely no help whatsoever, you'll never be disappointed.

CHAPTER 3

EAT OR BE EATEN

Young kids are picky eaters. If it isn't a plate of chicken nuggets or pizza, it's basically poison. Children are prepared to starve to death before they'll touch food that isn't precisely the right flavor. It's a hunger strike without purpose or principle, and no force on earth can stop it. Give me pepperoni or give me death.

None of this will change when the zombies come. Kids will demand their favorite foods long after the nation depletes its precious reserves of breaded bird chunks. In the opening moments of the apocalypse, the food supply chain will break down. The groceries in stock right then will be the last edible goods most retailers will ever get. Panicked shoppers will grab whatever they can carry, leaving store shelves stocked only with the stuff that wasn't worth looting. Good luck getting a kid to eat pork tongue and extruded beet paste. Be sure to loot some ketchup.

SAVVY SHOPPER

Your last grocery trip ever will also be your most important. You'll have to grab enough food to last the rest of your life, and what you bring home will determine how long or short that life will be. Hoard any food you can, no matter how much it makes your kids gag. If it's edible, it goes in the cart. Resist the urge to share with other shoppers. It'll only get you killed. Altruism is just a sappy form of suicide.

Head for the organic section first. The food there isn't any better, but the people who eat it are thoughtful and socially conscious. That makes them weak. Shove that vegan hipster aside and take the last head of locally grown cabbage. The worst he'll do to you is write a huffy post on social media. He won't survive the blackout.

Chances are all the good stuff will be gone long before you get there. Serves you right for sleeping in at the end of the world. Honestly, the grocery store shouldn't be your first stop anyway. While everyone else is preoccupied with getting the food they need to stay alive, head to the liquor store. Nobody will be there. It's a 100-percent-off sale, and everything must go. I am so looking forward to the apocalypse.

Looting a healthy assortment of food isn't hard. As always, the real challenge is getting your kids to eat it. Their very survival depends on it, but that won't make them take a single bite. It's possible they won't want to live in a world where pizza is extinct. I respect that decision.

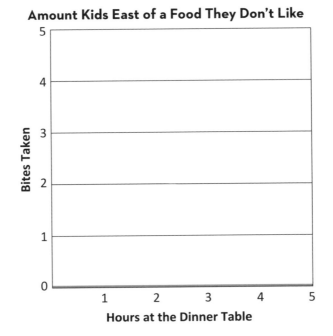

Amount Kids East of a Food They Don't Like

Bites Taken / Hours at the Dinner Table

FREEZER PARTY

It's best to ease your kids into survival-mode cuisine. I recommend kicking off your post-apocalyptic subsistence lifestyle with a huge feast of almost-expired food. Without electricity, everything in your fridge and freezer will spoil anyway. Let your kids eat anything they want. This is your chance to make the world's first and last sherbet hot dog casserole. Round out the meal with a snow cone salad and a hearty glass of chocolate syrup. That's the kind of whimsical, lighthearted fare you can only find at the mass extinction of humanity. Your kids will enjoy a brief moment of happiness followed by a lifetime of crushing disappointment. But that's how the world has always worked.

This final junk food binge isn't a shallow attempt to get your kids to quit whining for a few hours, although that's certainly a side benefit. It's actually a vital step toward survival. Like a bear preparing to hibernate for the winter, you need to build up your family's fat stores to endure the food shortages to come. Parents are uniquely well suited to this task. The pounds you've put on since you gave up on life will carry you through months of zombie-induced famine. Your stomach has been stretched by oversized portions and all-you-can-eat buffets. It's time to eat as much as humanly possible and then go back for thirds. The survival of our species depends on it. An entire lifetime of poor eating habits has been leading up to this moment. Those fit, healthy models on the magazine covers will be the first to die. The fat shall inherit the earth.

WHAT'S FOR DINNER?

Eventually, your kids will wake up from their food comas hungry and irritable. The banquet you gave them will instantly be forgotten. The only long-term memory children have is the grudges they'll have against you for their ruined childhoods. The good news is there won't be any therapists left to blame everything on you. People who help others are always the first to die. Serves them right.

After the final feast, the menu at dinnertime will be decidedly bleaker. Meals will consist of whatever will fill up your stomach without killing you. Admittedly, that's the standard I've always used for my cooking. I take "almost edible" as a compliment.

It's important to accept that this really is the best you can do for yourself and your kids. There's no point in uprooting your family to search for food elsewhere. The only thing worse than almost starving at home is almost starving on an endless road trip with a vehicle full of kids. After enough miles, you'll hope the zombies eat you just to end it.

The idea that there will be food somewhere else, especially in the countryside, is a myth anyway. Zombies will turn cities into devastated wastelands. Rural areas will just be devastated wastelands with more elbow room. When the zombies attack, food will be scarce everywhere, even on farms. The majority of tillable acreage in America is tied up in field corn, which is inedible to humans in its natural form, and soybeans, which are poisonous if eaten raw. Chowing down on either food without running it through a processing plant first is a bad idea unless you want to spend the rest of the apocalypse in a bathroom. Keep in mind there's a finite supply of toilet paper.

Even if catastrophic bowel movements are your idea of a good time, the harvest would be a one-time deal. There won't be enough fuel left for tractors to plant and then bring in thousands of bushels of crops. Fields will turn into giant, unkempt yards full of tall grasses, weeds, and hidden zombies. Avoid these at all costs. They're the perfect place to lose a child or a Frisbee.

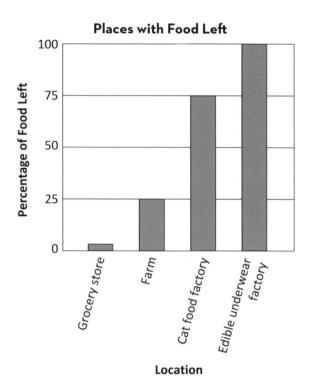

Places with Food Left

Percentage of Food Left (y-axis: 0, 25, 50, 75, 100)

Location (x-axis: Grocery store, Farm, Cat food factory, Edible underwear factory)

The only farms with the potential to provide food beyond the initial outbreak are the ones with livestock. Expect those to quickly be overrun by hungry, armed survivors with no idea how to raise animals. If there's not enough food for humans, there won't be for any other species, either. Starved, desperate animals will battle clueless looters on more or less even footing. Don't be shocked if pigs come out of this as the dominant species on earth. Keep your family far away from the fray. It's better to starve at home than to die being outsmarted by a walking pork chop.

URBAN GARDNER

Once the apocalypse begins, the only ones eating meat will be the zombies. The undead devour farm animals, too, so it's a bad idea to keep livestock around. Chickens, pigs, cows, and goats make more noise than children and are harder to control, although in terms of smell they're roughly equal. Putting animals in your backyard will attract a swarm of zombies who will stick around to eat you when they're done. They're ungrateful dinner guests. That leaves parents with only two options: Raise livestock inside your house or become vegetarians by default. Unless your spouse is more tolerant than mine on the issue of indoor manure piles, meat is officially off the menu. Cross your fingers that all the vegetarians in your life are already dead or you'll never hear the end of it.

Don't commit seppuku because there's no more bacon. The world ended. You don't deserve to be happy anymore. Your kids won't notice a difference anyway. The only meat they eat is hot dogs, and that doesn't come from any animal currently known to science.

Resist the temptation to eat the animals you already have. Murdering a beloved family pet and serving it for dinner isn't the best way to win your children's trust. Also, it would teach your kids an unfortunate lesson about how you treat family members when they're no longer useful. Remember that if you want to end up in a nursing home and not on a buffet table. And even if you make the mistake of slaying a cat or dog, your children won't eat it. They'll be so traumatized they probably won't eat anything ever again. That's great if you want to save on your grocery bill but less than ideal if you want your kids to stay alive. It's your call.

Just because you aren't going to eat your pets doesn't necessarily mean you should keep them around forever. A pet is an extra mouth to feed in a time of famine. The best plan is to discreetly turn them loose to fend for themselves some night after the kids go to sleep. When your children ask, don't make up some stupid lie about sending the family dog to a farm. Instead, make up a better lie about sending your animals to pet college. That will also explain why there's no money to send your own kids to people college on the off chance the world gets up and running again.

With all options for meat exhausted, it's time to start gardening. The good news is there'll be plenty of land available. With the collapse of Western civilization, your neighbors won't be around to vigilantly police their property lines. Feel free to annex nearby yards as needed. First do a courtesy knock on your neighbors' front doors to make sure they're dead. Have a weapon handy to kill them if they've turned. Don't kill them if they're still human, though. That's un-neighborly, not to mention a violation of homeowner's association codes.

To grow a garden in the apocalypse, pick vegetables that are both kid-proof and zombie-proof. Both are likely to march through your garden and trample your produce, but neither will stop to eat it. The undead will have little interest in your crops. In fact, they can help out by eating pests like deer and rabbits. Unfortunately, they'll also want to eat you. Zombies, like children, take everything too far. The key to a successful garden is to work *with* zombies, not against them. Tie up a few around the garden. Make sure the restraints are long enough that the zombies can still grab varmints but short enough they can't grab you. It's not something to test out through trial and error. One mistake and you'll be torn limb from limb by an undead monster. But on the plus side, your rhubarb will look spectacular.

EATING SADNESS

Once the garden is surrounded by a precarious ring of hungry corpses, it's time to plant. There are benefits and drawbacks to each type of vegetable. Choose wisely.

Vegetable	Pro	Con
Sweet Corn	It's tall, so you can jump out from behind it and scare people.	Scaring people might end poorly when everyone is armed.
Potatoes	They're underground, so it's hard for kids or zombies to trample them.	Any potato that isn't vodka has failed to live up to its true potential.
Pumpkins	They're great for pie.	Your kids will insist on carving them into jack-o'-lanterns instead of eating them even as you all starve to death.
Peas	Technically, they're food.	Feeding them to kids is borderline child abuse.
Green Beans	They're green; they're beans. What do you want from me?	Not recommended for people with working taste buds.
Carrots	They take a long time to eat, which is good if you're on a diet.	Dieting is the opposite of what you're going for here. Also, they don't help your eyes. Like you needed one more letdown in your life.
Cabbage	It's better than eating razorblades, I guess.	Occasionally it turns into a doll of dubious collector's value.
Lettuce	It goes great with burgers.	Cows will go extinct on the first day of the zombie apocalypse. Also, lettuce is paper in plant form.
Cucumbers	They're a great opportunity for penis jokes.	Marital strain caused by too many penis jokes.
Zucchini	I don't even know what this is.	Fire?

Rest assured, kids aren't any more likely to eat vegetables from your backyard than they are from a grocery store. It's good to know planting a garden, like all other parenting efforts, is ultimately futile.

However, there are a few tricks you can use to incentivize vegetable consumption and keep your kids miserable but alive. That's always been your best-case scenario as a parent.

✓ **Do** force your children to eat. Shove the vegetables in their mouths if you have to. You're bigger than them. Might makes right.

✗ **Don't** give your kids a choice. Never ask them what they want. Tell them what they'll have. It's a short walk from options to insurrection.

✓ **Do** make them eat it all. Anything children say in an attempt to leave the table early is a lie. No one has ever been full halfway through a radish.

✗ **Don't** negotiate with terrorists. Never bribe them to discourage bad behavior. You have the power. It's your way or starvation.

✓ **Do** lie to them. Offer them all sorts of wonderful things if they finish their food. This is different than negotiating with terrorists because you won't keep any of your promises.

✗ **Don't** tell the truth. Dishonesty is so important I put it on here twice. Tell your kids zombies can hear rumbling stomachs, and suddenly that expired can of refried beans doesn't sound so bad.

✓ **Do** eat the leftovers. If you fail to get your kids to eat—which you probably will—scarf down whatever remains. One of you might as well survive.

✘ **Don't** apologize. You didn't cause the chicken nugget shortage. Even if, in the eyes of your children, that will always be your fault, just like everything else in the world.

✔ **Do** eat the ugly vegetables. This isn't a beauty contest. Weird, deformed vegetables with bad spots are just as nutritious as vegetables that look good. Okay, that's a lie. No vegetables look good.

✘ **Don't** give your kids false hope. There are no better meals around the corner. The world sucks. No need to sugarcoat it, especially since mentioning sugar would just make them hungrier.

THE MAGIC BAG OF WONDER

If there's one thing little kids love more than chicken nuggets and pizza, it's dog food. It's like crack to toddlers. If there's any of it in your house or any other house in a three-state radius, your kids will find and eat it the second you look away. Let them. You won't need it for your dog since he'll be off at pet college. Hopefully he's not wasting your money on a liberal arts degree.

While dog food isn't meant for human consumption, it must have at least some nutritional value for tiny humans. Kids and dogs aren't all that different. They both roll around on the ground and look super cute until they poop on your floor. I say let your kids eat it and see what happens. But before you go that route, be sure state governments have totally broken down. Otherwise things will get awkward when Child Protective Services show up.

FLOWER OF LIFE

If you want to stay alive, think like a toddler. They're great at eating all kinds of things that aren't technically edible but also won't kill them. The colorful modeling dough children play with falls in that category. It's not meant for human consumption, yet there are multiple accessories to shape it into hamburgers and spaghetti. It's the same sort of encouragement-by-discouragement cigarette companies use when they say kids shouldn't smoke because they're not old enough to look that cool. Modeling compounds shouldn't be a regular meal, but it's okay for an occasional treat. Your kids are going to eat it anyway, and it'll keep away their hunger pangs for a while. Plus it will make their poop look amazing.

Your dough supply will run out eventually, even if you're the only survivor who bothered to loot it. Fortunately there's an even better source of fiber that grows in your own backyard: dandelions. The first instinct of small children is to stick everything in their mouths. Instead of stopping them, just sit back and wait. Don't watch them too closely, though. Otherwise they'll suspect you approve and will immediately stop doing it. Instead, expressly forbid your kids from eating dandelions ahead of time. Your children will graze your yard free of weeds within minutes. Dandelions don't have much to offer in terms of calories, but at least you'll have the nicest lawn of the apocalypse.

FINISH YOUR FOOD

Kids are suicidally stubborn. Convincing them to clean their plates is nearly impossible, and zombies won't change that. It'll take something more substantial than the end of the world to give your children an attitude adjustment. Stick with it, however, and with any luck your children will survive. And if they don't, well, they'll come back as zombies. At least then they'll finally have a healthy appetite.

CHAPTER 4

WHAT'S YOURS IS MINE

The zombie apocalypse won't be all bad. Sure, billions of people will die, but there won't be any more infomercials, road construction, or surprise visits from your in-laws. It'll also be a golden age for looting. You'll be able to take anything you want—assuming someone else doesn't kill you to take it back. When you break in and seize stuff, you won't be a criminal; you'll be a survivor. You'll get to seek out your own personal enrichment AND have the moral high ground. What a time to be alive.

Once the smashing and grabbing starts, you and your children will finally have something in common. Acquiring stuff that isn't yours is a natural human instinct. Never, since the birth of the human race, have little kids respected the personal property of others. Sharing is a learned behavior forced on the young to make them comply with the arbitrary standards of society. Taking, well, that comes naturally.

Looting is the perfect bonding activity for parents and kids. As a mom or dad, you have the knowledge necessary to quickly locate and carry back survival supplies. Kids, meanwhile, have the small size and endless energy to check all the nooks and crannies you might overlook. When motivated by the prospect of personal gain, kids can keep going forever. Just make sure whatever you loot is sugar-free.

SHOP TILL YOU DROP AND REANIMATE

To prevent your kids from getting morally confused, don't call your supply runs "looting." Call them "shopping" and then never pay for anything. Children don't understand how money works, anyway. Your kids won't ask any questions as long as they get free stuff.

Shopping with kids is perilous in normal times. In the zombie apocalypse it'll get easier. If your kids break something in the middle of a store, you won't have to buy it. When they steal stuff, no one will call the police. And no matter how badly your kids behave, there won't be anyone left to judge your family. The fact that your kids are alive at all is a testament to your superior parenting skills—or random luck or zombie incompetence. Take your pick. But in the unlikely event you do encounter someone who judges you, don't feel bad. Just rob them.

HOLE IN THE WALL

When scavenging for supplies, target out-of-the-way venues unlikely to attract either humans or zombies. Small businesses that always seem on the verge of closing are a great choice. Everyone ignored those "shop local" campaigns before the world ended, and there's no reason that'll change now. Capitalism is every bit as mindless and cruel as the undead.

It's a little extra work to take your kids on these expeditions, but it'll pay off in the long run. Children are less likely to complain about whatever you bring home if they have a choice. They don't, but your goal is to make them think they do. The illusion of free will stops humanity from spiraling into a vortex of nihilistic despair. Let your kids choose between two dented, unlabeled cans of mystery foodstuffs. Then when they're not looking, throw both cans in the cart. If your children think they picked it out, they'll be more likely to eat whatever is inside. They'll have no one to blame for the awful taste but themselves, though they'll still direct their anger at you. That's how kids work.

When you're on a supply run, don't let your kids out of your sight. Even if you stick to relatively safe looting spots, there could always be a stray zombie trapped in a bathroom somewhere. There are worse places to spend eternity. I'm looking at you, Minnesota during mosquito season. Keep your kids within arm's reach so you can pull them out of harm's way if necessary, but let them forage on their own within that radius. That leaves them free to crawl around on the ground and look for low stuff you might have missed.

It's always possible a box or can of food got knocked down when the initial wave of looters went through. Kids can also bend down and retrieve stray items while you remain upright. Your knees and back will thank you for this brilliant arrangement, even if your kids never do.

As an added incentive, let your kids keep any money they find. Coins will be useless in the zombie apocalypse, but your children will feel like they came out ahead. This will make them more likely to risk their lives to help you find food. Just don't let them eat any coins or stick them up their noses. That seems like common sense, but it's not. Ingested pennies kill more kids every year than zombies ever will.

MEALS ON WHEELS

Whenever possible, use a shopping cart. It will let you haul more stuff, and in an emergency you can toss your kids in it and use it as a getaway vehicle. Plus, if you get a running start, you can jump on the back to glide effortlessly through stores. Unless the cart is empty or you're fat, in which case it'll tip over backward and your spouse will glower at you for the rest of the shopping trip. Not that that's ever happened to me or anything.

Don't leave the shopping cart behind when you exit the store. It makes an excellent zombie battering ram, or so I've deduced from watching my kids push one. It's certainly effective at knocking over store displays and other shoppers. If you live nearby, push the cart all the way home. If you don't, toss the entire cart in the back of your vehicle. Packing individual items in your trunk in the middle of an exposed parking lot is an open invitation for an attack. Don't expect zombies to warn you with an RSVP. Of course, a shopping cart well-laden with looted goods will be too heavy to lift. You'll only be able to hoist it up if you fail as a gatherer. If my track record pre-apocalypse is any indication, I'll be able to lift it every time.

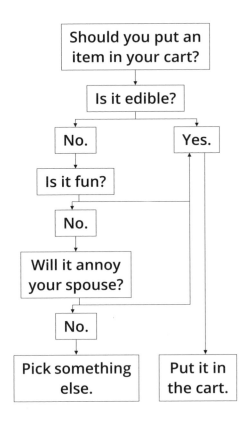

SAME AS CASH

It will only take looters a matter of hours to strip popular stores of nearly all valuable provisions. Traveling around from one big box retailer to the next will be dangerous and inefficient. Everyone else will do the same thing, and where there are people, there are zombies. The only food in those stores will be you.

Instead of seeking out food, target a durable good you can trade for it. The item you choose has to be universally in demand but in short supply. To make sure the market doesn't get flooded, it has to be something the post-apocalyptic world can't make. And finally, it has to be something everyone else will overlook so you have a chance to snatch it up before the rest of humanity realizes its mistake. There's only one item that fits all those criteria. I'm talking, of course, about diapers.

When I say diapers, I mean the disposable kind. Cloth diapers are a bad idea, regardless of the zombie situation. Throwing away a regular diaper takes ten seconds, but with cloth diapers, you have to spend hours washing, sanitizing, and drying them. That should be fun without working appliances. The only upside of cloth diapers is they're supposedly better for the environment. But once the apocalypse hits, there won't be any environment left to save. Zombies will eat everything cute and cuddly, and the only animals left will be the ones nobody cares about. No one is going to reuse dirty poop rags to save the garter snakes.

In the zombie apocalypse, cloth diapers won't be a pillar of green activism; they'll be a sign of poverty. Survivors who are "rich"—the ones with the resources to live lives of relative ease compared to the rest of humanity—will use regular disposable diapers. The fundamental human condition is to be sick of dealing with other people's crap. That's literally what changing a diaper is. Anything that makes that process simpler will be as valuable as food or water. The joy of not having your house smell like baby poop is priceless—except on the free market, where it'll have an exact monetary value.

Diaper Value Estimates

Quantity of Diapers	Trade Value
1	Five cans of food, a six-pack of warm beer, or 2,000 old issues of *National Geographic* someone's aunt saved in her attic because she thought they'd be worth something someday but now they're just a fire hazard.
10	Fifty cans of food, a top-of-the-line racing bike with only a little bit of duct tape on the seat, or one can of cold beer that someone chilled by rowing out to an iceberg.
20	A pig, rent for one month in a medium-size New York apartment in a neighborhood where you may or may not get murdered, or an inflatable bounce house that you'll have to blow up yourself since the fan won't work anymore.
50	Someone's first-born child, the *Mona Lisa* plus a marker so you can sign it and say it's by you, or an entire two-ton army truck full of cheese puffs. Somebody looted right.
100	Dowry for a new husband or wife (clear this with your current spouse first), the Empire State Building, or a horse that can stomp its foot the right number of times to answer basic math questions.
1,000	A duchy along with all associated lands and titles, a horse that can do calculus, or the world's last bag of chocolate chips. I recommend option three.

Even when the value of diapers is at its peak, you'll still let babies poop in them. Without that basic function, diapers will be useless. Plus it'll feel good.

It'll be like lighting a cigar with a hundred-dollar bill, but only if you destroyed the mint first so no other hundred-dollar bills could ever be created. With every dump a baby takes, your currency supply will diminish, but all remaining diapers will become more valuable. The last diaper on earth could buy an entire country. Too bad that country will be filled with walking corpses.

Childless people will hoard diapers, too. Even if they don't ever plan on having kids, a diaper stockpile will give them a bargaining chip to use with parents. The pool of potential customers is the entire human race. Parenthood can strike anyone without warning. Well, technically there are forty weeks of warning, but it still takes people by surprise somehow. Once the world ends, the only birth control method will be pulling out. If I had a kid for every time that didn't work, I'd have four. Whether for trade or as a precaution against future life events, everyone will need diapers. They'll be more valuable than gold and a lot easier to carry around. Good luck hauling gold bullion in a diaper bag.

CURRENCY CONVERSION

As currency of the new barter-based economy, diapers aren't perfect. For starters, they're great for changing babies, but they're bad for making change. If you buy something that's worth one and a half diapers, that half a diaper won't do anyone any good. You can't make a baby take half a bowel movement. And to be clear, I didn't mean that as a challenge. Please don't send me any pictures.

There are other goods survivors might use as a currency, but they won't work as well. The most likely candidate is toilet paper. The drawback there is while everyone needs it, it's easily replaceable. Serviceable substitutes include leaves, old newspapers, and pages from books. When the world ends, libraries will enjoy a sudden surge in popularity. Even dollar bills can make good toilet paper, which is ironic since toilet paper makes such poor money. Grab toilet paper when you can, but don't expect it to be effective on the barter scene. When it comes to professional transactions, use diapers if you want to be taken seriously.

ARMED AND UNHARMED

Some items in the zombie apocalypse won't be for sale, no matter how many diapers you have. No one will sell you a gun if you could use it to rob them and get your Pampers back. If you want tools of destruction, you'll have to loot them, but that approach is perilous at best. If you need to steal a weapon from someone, by definition that means they're armed and you aren't. That should end well. The only way your robbery will succeed is if you already have a better weapon than they do, which begs the question of why you bothered to steal from them in the first place. A weapon might be unguarded if its owner is already dead, but if that's the case you should leave it alone. It obviously didn't do the last guy any good.

Stay away from gun stores if you can help it. If the owner is alive, he'll shoot you, and if he's dead, his merchandise obviously sucks. Even if you know of an unguarded source of guns, it's still best not to loot them. Every time you fire a gun to kill one zombie, the noise will attract more. You'll have to shoot those, too, which will draw in even more of the undead. Your bullet supply will dwindle as the zombie horde grows larger and larger. Or you could skip using a gun altogether and go home and take a nap. It's your call.

If you really want to keep your family alive, loot bladed weapons instead. You don't have to reload a knife, unless it's some kind of weird hybrid knife-gun or gun-knife. One is a knife that shoots bullets, and the other is a gun that shoots knives. I might be making that up. Even I can't tell anymore. The only thing I know for sure is if everyone had one, the zombie apocalypse never would've happened. Knife-gun control laws doomed us all.

Most other slicing tools won't be that elaborate, but it's better that way. People are less likely to guard knives than guns because cutting utensils are common and cheap, like your mom. I apologize to any mothers I offended. Please don't stab me. In reality, it's almost impossible to avoid bladed weapon attacks. Knives are everywhere. Easy places to find them include retail stores, people's houses, and your own back. Unfortunately, metaphorical knives have little value for killing zombies.

Knives are handy because they were made to cut stuff. The same can't be said for swords. Most of the ones in stores are cheap knockoffs that'll break if you try to slice anything more deadly than fruit. By all means grab that cool-looking katana to hang up in your room, but only use it if you're attacked by a horde of angry cantaloupes.

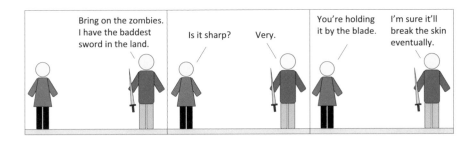

I COME BEARING GIFTS

The zombie apocalypse is the perfect time to become the parent you always pretended to be on the internet. Kids naturally want every single toy they see on a commercial. Previously, you never would've bought that stuff because you're a responsible adult with limited means. But once the world ends, anything goes. Other parents will be distracted looting survival necessities. Since you'll buy that stuff with diapers later, you won't have any competition when you snatch everything in the toy aisle. Material goods won't make your family happy, but neither will poverty. Grab everything you can and take your chances.

Once the world ends, there won't be a budget limit for turning your wish list into a reality. Impress your children by breaking into a jewelry display case and taking everything shiny. It should all still be there. No one will care about jewelry once the food shortages start. You can't eat gold, no matter how much hot sauce you use. Never accept jewelry in a trade, but feel free to loot it if you walk by a store. It's light, and kids like anything that sparkles. Your daughter will think you're the best parent ever when you casually toss her a sack with 1,000 carats of diamonds. Just make sure she doesn't drop them anyplace a baby might choke on them.

ALMOST FOOD

A healthy diaper stockpile will help you trade for food, but it won't be enough on its own. You can't rely entirely on trading to get what you need because eventually everyone else might run out of rations, too. At that point, you'll have to fall back on your own meager vegetable garden and whatever nonedible household items your kids are desperate enough to eat. Hide the decorative bath soaps.

If you must forage for your own food, skip the stores and head to the nearest fast food burger joint. You'll have the whole place to yourself. Rational people will assume the food there went bad without refrigeration. That's where they're wrong. Highly scientific studies conducted by random people posting pictures of their food on the internet show certain fast food burgers never, ever spoil. Some images show "beef" patties remaining unchanged for entire presidential administrations. Those sandwiches could outlast humanity itself. Cows will have the last laugh after all.

Nobody knows what's actually in these burgers, but just one has more calories than an entire steer. A single meal straight off the menu should feed your whole family for a week. Kids love fast food, so getting them to eat it won't be a problem. And yes, those burgers will slowly kill you, but that beats dying quickly from starvation. The best part is you don't need to do anything special to store them. Just cook them all on the first day and stack them in a cabinet like hockey pucks. Then enjoy eating one or two a day until a zombie eats you or your heart explodes, whichever comes first.

If you're not in the mood for burgers, loot other houses in the neighborhood. Everyone has some canned goods in the back of their cabinets that are virtually inedible even when brand new. These are what are known as "donor cans." Nobody remembers who bought them or why, but the only reason they'll ever leave that cabinet is if someone comes by asking for contributions for a food drive. Poor people probably like jalapeño tuna or concentrated sweet potato extract canned sometime in the early eighties. And if they don't, that's extra motivation for them to find a job.

At the start of the apocalypse, hit up the houses of your friends and neighbors and grab the donor cans as fast as possible. Your kids won't like the food inside, and neither will you. But nobody will shoot you when you loot it. They'll probably thank you for finally getting it out of their houses. Procuring these items won't be a problem, but actually eating them might be. You have to decide if you'd rather die by zombie bites or food poisoning. The zombie apocalypse is full of choices.

YESTERDAY'S FASHIONS, TODAY'S PRICES

Walking around naked in the zombie apocalypse is a bad idea. Yes, societal norms will fail along with society itself, but that doesn't mean you have to make the situation worse. People will see enough horrible things without having to catch a glimpse of your underwhelming genitalia. Besides, it'll be cold when the power cuts out. If you're a guy, you'll definitely want clothes to hide the shrinkage.

When looting clothes, stay away from the mall and head directly to secondhand stores. Absolutely no one will compete with you. Seriously, free isn't that much of a discount from their normal prices. Since no humans will be there, the place should be zombie-free. Grab sizes for your kids for every age between now and adulthood. Fill your vehicle with armloads of embarrassing, almost-wearable clothing. You don't want to make another trip. Anything you don't like you can burn for warmth or, depending on how tough times are, eat. Stay away from polyester. It's hard on the digestive tract.

THE TAKEAWAY

Looting will keep you alive and will genuinely be a lot of fun. Your kids will get a kick out of spending time with you and breaking every rule you taught them over the course of their lives. However, the thrill of this vigilantism will diminish over time, not because the fun of destruction is shallow and temporary, but because all the good stuff will be gone. Always look in places other people aren't interested in. One man's trash is another man's family dinner for four.

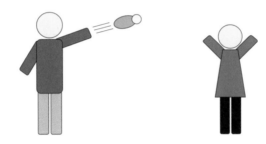

CHAPTER 5

GOING THE DISTANCE

When dealing with any crisis, you have three options:

1. Run.
2. Hide.
3. Fight.

Those are the steps law enforcement agencies teach for dealing with active shooters, but they also apply for shepherding children through the zombie apocalypse. Two-thirds of those options are ways of defusing a situation by sidestepping conflict. The best way to solve any situation is to avoid it forever. That's the lesson I learned from my marriage. I loaded the dishwasher wrong one time two years ago. My wife still can't find me.

As a parent, the "run" option is most important to master. It's the one you'll use the most often and also requires the least amount of thought. It's so easy it's a problem. If you ever notice your feet moving when you didn't tell them to, it means your body took over because your brain was too slow and stupid to figure out what to do. Nobody knows you better than you. If you were young and single, fleeing by yourself in blind terror would be fine, but you have kids. Don't leave them behind to be eaten alive. They take it personally.

If you and your family are going to survive the zombie apocalypse, you'll have to learn to flee together. Running away the right way is a mix of art and science with a dash of total panic sprinkled in. This approach won't resolve any of your problems. But it will keep you a step ahead of them for one more day.

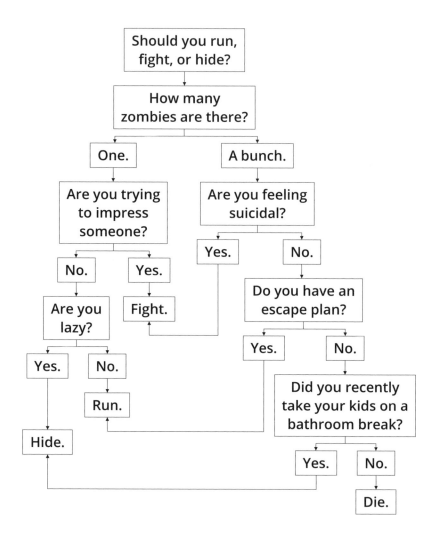

ON THE RUN

Running is the natural choice for anyone, but especially parents. Your survival instincts tell you to dodge confrontation now and deal with the fallout later. It's the same reason you tell your kids "maybe" when you mean "no." By avoiding danger, you live to fight another day. Actually, that defeats the purpose. You live to run away another day. There's no shame in that. Zombies can't bite what they can't catch, except in the nightmare scenario where they have dentures and learn to throw them. Let's not give them any ideas.

For the purposes of this guide, the term "running" covers all methods of moving away from zombies. It doesn't necessarily have to be a sprint. It could mean tiptoeing, crawling, or even dancing. Just make sure you don't pick anything louder than a foxtrot. Tap dancing will get you killed.

PACE SETTER

The best way to run from zombies is not to run at all. A brisk walk is usually fast enough. For reference, imagine the speed you'd need to outpace your elderly grandmother. I don't know why you'd ever want to do that, but picture it anyway. Maybe there's only one piece of hard candy left and you never learned to share. As long as you move at a steady rate, you should be able to stay ahead of her. Just don't stand still for too long or she'll punch you in the gut and steal your candy. If a woman in her eighties wants something badly enough to race for it, she'll definitely resort to violence. It's a good thing this isn't the old people apocalypse. There'd be no survivors.

Kids can comfortably maintain a brisk walk, but anything faster than that and your family might get separated. As every horror movie ever made demonstrates, splitting up cuts your odds of survival to zero. Inevitably, a zombie will grab one kid, and the rest of the family will attempt to save them. It's not a rational decision, but parents have a sentimental attachment to their children. The few seconds you saved by speeding up will be more than negated by your entire family getting massacred. It's hard to get anywhere on time when you're dead.

Running from zombies is more about situational awareness and path-finding than speed. The undead don't have to be fast to catch your family. They're a threat because they outnumber you and never give up. It's the same

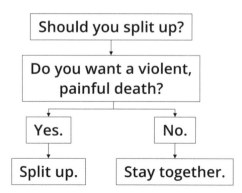

reason your kids usually get what they want. If zombies slowly close in on you from all sides without ever stopping to take a break, it's likely one of them will snag you. But as long as you keep your family moving and watch out for spots where you might get cornered, you should live long enough to die from something non–zombie related. Old age is a pipe dream, but there are other good ways to go. I'm still hoping to fatally overdose on cotton candy.

SPEED DEMON

Even when you're by yourself, actually running is a bad idea. You'll put increased distance between yourself and an individual zombie, but you'll eventually have to stop. When you do, there will be zombies at your new location, too. They'll be everywhere. It's the zombie apocalypse, not the zombie occasional sighting. By exhausting yourself, you'll do the zombies a massive favor by making yourself easier to catch. Don't expect any gratitude, though. They'll tear you apart without so much as a thank-you card.

There will be times, however, when a leisurely stroll won't do. Perhaps a wall of zombies is closing in on you and a quick dash is the only way to escape. Or maybe your spouse has a headache and a quick trip to loot some over-the-counter medicine is the only way you'll get laid. Whatever the reason, if you must run, keep these dos and don'ts in mind:

✓ **Do** wear the right footwear. It's hard to outrun anything in high heels. Plus if you come back as a zombie, you'll be doomed to an eternity of calluses.

✗ **Don't** stretch. You should only run in an emergency. If you have time to stretch, you have time to slack off and walk.

✓ **Do** watch where you're going. It doesn't do any good to dodge one zombie if you run directly into another. That would be embarrassing and also fatal.

✖ **Don't** forget to look down. You don't want to step on a prone zombie and die—or, even worse, end up tracking zombie splatter into your house.

✓ **Do** stiff-arm zombies liberally. They are poorly balanced and will fall over easily.

✖ **Don't** make fake crowd noises while you do it. Pretend you're winning the Heisman Trophy if you must. Just keep the sound effects to a minimum.

✖ **Don't** be discouraged if your oldest kids are faster than you and leave you in the dust. It's better to have living children than sappy, attached ones.

✓ **Do** quit as soon as you can. There isn't a prize for going farther. Nobody is impressed by that "26.2" sticker on the back of your minivan.

Most children who are old enough to walk are fast enough to dodge a zombie. However, a young kid's top speed is irrelevant because they don't have the attention span to keep it up. Little kids will stop to look at a cool rock. Or to backtrack to see another rock that might have been even cooler. Or to complain you didn't give them enough time to compare the two. Small children either need to be herded or carried. For that reason, I recommend at least one adult per every two children. At the very least, you have two hands, so you can grab both kids and drag them along while they throw temper tantrums. It'll be just like when you took them to the grocery store in the pre-apocalypse world, only you'll die of zombie bites instead of public humiliation.

When moving multiple young children, keep them in a group. You can't protect them if they're scattered. And inevitably, they'll do everything in their power to go in different directions. It's like herding cats, only kids talk back and have sharper claws. Trimming their nails won't get any easier when the world ends.

There are a few proven parenting methods to keep kids together, but they're not for everyone. Only use these tricks if you want your children to live.

Ways to Keep Track of Children When on the Move

Method	Pro	Con
Holding Hands in a Long Chain	You can break apart at a moment's notice if necessary.	Kids will fight constantly and attract every zombie on the planet.
Tying Everyone Together with Mountaineering Rope	There's no way to get lost.	Turns your family into interconnected sausage links.
Child Leashes	Children will always be within a few feet of you.	Demeaning to everyone involved.
Buddy System	You gain more accountability by pairing children to watch each other.	A great way to lose two kids at once.
Sheepdog	Good enough to herd livestock, good enough to herd your kids.	Only helpful after your kids fall down a well.
Hypnosis	Puts your kids in a trance so they follow all commands to stay close.	Kids may or may not believe they are poultry.

Walkie-Talkies	You can communicate with kids out of visual range to make sure they come back.	Kids and husbands will play with them and forget why they left home in the first place.
Matching T-shirts	If your kids get separated, other survivors will know they belong to you.	Kids will be so ashamed they'll wander away on purpose.

ALL ABOARD

When it comes to lugging small children around, nothing beats a piggyback ride. By keeping your offspring directly on top of you, you'll minimize their chances to get themselves killed. They won't make it easy for you. Backpackers know that after a few miles even a light load feels heavy. This is doubly true when the load wiggles and whines the whole time. The hardest part will be not dropping them on purpose.

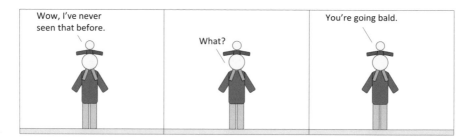

The ideal piggyback rider is big enough to support some of their own weight without being so big you can't hold them up. Make sure they stick out their arms as far as they can. Otherwise they'll end up bear-hugging your neck, which is a good way to suddenly black out. If you're in the process of training your kids to do jujitsu, that rear naked choke is a plus. But if there's a pack of zombies pursuing you, falling to the floor unconscious is a little inconvenient.

As hard as piggyback rides are, they're still better than carrying children in your arms. Kids are heavy. A toddler who doesn't want to be lifted weighs as much as lead and is just as deadly. Prolonged exposure to either one will make your hair fall out. Toddlers will exhaust your arms or back, but letting kids of that size stand on their own is out of the question. They walk so slowly they practically move backward. The only exception is if they're doing something they're not supposed to. Then they're blurs of light that break the sound barrier.

If a situation deteriorates and you can't carry a small child any farther, stash them someplace secure while you stand and fight the pursuing horde. The goal is to neutralize just enough zombies to buy you a little space before you start running again. Killing a monster or two and getting a quick breather could save your life, not because the zombies will no longer be able to bite you, but because you need the rest to avoid a heart attack. Like many parents, I'm horribly out of shape. Kids are the best excuse for not going to the gym. It's the main reason I had them.

To stash your young children, look for a location where you can temporarily trap them to prevent them from running away. You won't come across many fully assembled playpens in the apocalypse, so you'll have to improvise. The best solution in a pinch is a park trash can. They're too tall and heavy for a toddler to climb out of or tip over. Plus they're full of garbage. You've spent years telling your kids not to eat trash, so letting them munch on whatever they want should keep them quiet for a few minutes. Hopefully their shots are up to date. Just don't forget your kids in the trash can when you leave. It takes forever to make new ones.

Top Places to Temporarily Trap a Toddler When Zombies Attack

Location	Pro	Con
Under a Clothes Basket	Lots of air holes.	You'll have to weigh it down with something heavy. Might crush the basket and the toddler.
Random Fenced-In Yard	They're everywhere.	Might contain zombies or dog poop.
Cardboard Box	Kids love these.	You might be tempted to add stamps and mail them.
Random Room in the Building You're In	Easy to toss a kid in and close the door.	Might forget where you put them.
On a Tree Branch	Your kid probably won't jump down.	If you can reach, so can the undead. It's an elevated zombie feeder.
In an Abandoned Vehicle	Zombies can't open car doors.	Kids will ruin the upholstery.
On Top of an Abandoned Vehicle	Gives your child an excellent vantage point from which to watch you fight.	They'll finally realize how bad you are at everything.

At the Top of a Twirly Slide	Built-in escape route if zombies climb the stairs.	Kids will circle back and go down the slide again and again.

LIMITED POTENTIAL

Before you leave home with your children, you need a realistic idea of how far and fast you can travel on foot. This is true even if you have a vehicle. Cars get stuck or break down all the time. Once the world ends, there won't be any mechanics to tell you that you need a thirty-five-cent part with $500 in labor. The zombie apocalypse is a bad time for a cross-country road trip. Sorry if your kids had their hearts set on a vacation to an abandoned, zombie-infested amusement park. It would probably still be too expensive.

Try to keep all trips under ten miles. That way you at least have a chance to make it home if you have to flee on foot. If you draw that radius out from your house, that gives you roughly 300 square miles to scavenge in. If you can't loot enough to survive in an area that size, your standard of living is too high for the end of the world. Cut back on the caviar, and save the good toilet paper for company.

The size of the radius you can draw will depend on your individual level of endurance. There are some people who make physical fitness a priority even after they have children. These people are mysterious unicorns powered by dark magic. Avoid them at all costs. For the rest of us, moving long distances on foot will be a nightmare. As a parent, traveling one mile forward will require three miles of walking as you weave between children to break up fights, wipe noses, and backtrack to pick up stragglers. All this fruitless exercise will force you to get in shape without generating much forward progress. At least the zombies will be grateful. Lean meat is easier to chew than fat.

ROLLING DOOM

Luckily, ancient man invented a simple tool to solve this problem. No, I'm not talking about the inclined plane, although I love a good ramp as much as the next guy. The solution here is the wheel. You won't have to waste energy herding your kids as you retreat if you can push them where you want them to go. This is especially handy if one of them is injured or uncooperative for no reason at all. A toddler's temper tantrum is much less likely to get you killed if you can toss them on a cart like a sack of potatoes and move on with your life.

Best Ways to Push Children

Wheeled Device	Pro	Con
Stroller	Has straps to hold in little kids.	Roll bars and crash helmets cost extra.
Shopping Cart	Also holds the stuff you loot.	Comes straight from the factory with one bad wheel.
Wheelbarrow	Kids are lighter than mounds of dirt.	Prone to tipping over when children are onboard. Slightly more serious than spilling mulch.

Hand Cart	Great for moving boxes.	Kids are seldom box-shaped.
Red Wagon	Nostalgia.	Rickety metal wheels are the only things on earth louder than your kids.
Trashcan on Wheels	With the lid on, you won't hear them complain.	Kids will require extra baths.
Skateboard	Kids can propel themselves.	They'll break a leg trying something stupid they saw on the internet.
Janitor's Mop Bucket	Kid who stands in it will get a bonus foot cleaning.	Will really piss off the janitor.

RUN AWAY

Parents are masters of the tactical retreat. Whether it's a backyard barbecue or a shopping mall full of carnivorous corpses, moms and dads know how to feign an excuse and leave early before their kids break anything valuable. As a parent, you've been running away all your adult life. The only difference during the zombie apocalypse is it'll make you a survivor, not a social pariah. Remember: If in doubt, run away. It's the bravest thing you can do.

CHAPTER 6

HIDE AND GO WEEP

Running isn't always the answer. Sometimes it's better to shelter in place and wait for zombies to leave on their own. I use similar tactics against my children. If I dodge them for long enough, they'll wander away and bother someone else. Like most adults, I spend the majority of my day fading into the background in the hope no one will notice I exist. All good parents are at least half chameleon.

The real challenge will be teaching this skill to your children. Hiding combines the fun of being quiet with the excitement of sitting still. It's the ultimate game of hide and seek against opponents who are literally brain dead. To win, all you have to do is stop fidgeting and shut up for a while.

Kids are capable of neither. As an adult, you know you should be virtually catatonic if you're hiding in a closet with zombies right outside the door. But to a kid, that's the perfect time to loudly ask you about your favorite animal. At that moment, it'll be a bear since they eat their young.

BAD TO THE BONE

Little kids are naturally terrible hiders. Thousands of years without any real predators wrecked their survival skills. Other species developed speed and camouflage to avoid being eaten, but *Homo sapiens* children didn't have anything to fear. Our ancestors systematically wiped out every animal that posed a threat. Or was annoying. Or was fun to kill. Honestly, we went a little overboard, but better safe than sorry. For all we know, dodos could've eaten babies or something.

For much of human history, being good at hiding was a detriment. Most parents don't pay close attention to their children. A kid who is good at evading detection would be left behind. As the centuries passed, children found ways to be so stupidly obvious even the most grudging parents couldn't pretend to forget about them. Today, little kids hide behind couches with only their heads covered or under tables where they're visible for a full 360 degrees. Their goal isn't to conceal themselves; it's to be adorably incompetent. Parents are much more likely to feed a cute child than a stealthy one. This strategy worked brilliantly until real predators returned to the scene.

Things Children Fail at on Purpose

Skill	Reason They Fail
Hiding	Makes them adorable. Harder to give them up for adoption.
Folding Laundry	Turns you into their personal maid until they're adults.
Tying Shoes	Forces you to kneel down before them. Know your place.
Sharing	Lets them be selfish jerks for as long as possible.
Walking	Using your own legs is for suckers.
Potty Training	Nothing beats the convenience of pooping in the middle of the living room.
Dishes	If they stall for long enough, you'll buy a dishwasher.
Downloading Games	They can always pretend they bought that app "by accident."

It's delightful when toddlers "hide" behind curtains with their feet still sticking out, but only until they get eaten right in front of you.

The first kids who were bad at hiding did it on purpose, but now children can't help it. When it comes to this skill and many others, incompetence is hardwired into their systems. That silence you hear is millions of public school teachers not being surprised at all.

It's hard to imagine how kids could be any worse at hiding. They pick a bad spot the first time and then use it over and over again. Yes, kid, everyone sees you behind that inch-and-a-half-wide broom handle. But go ahead and hide there six more times and I'll act shocked because it's easier than searching the house to find you somewhere else. Bad hiding spots are offensive to everybody involved. When you're looking for a kid and they hide behind a clear glass aquarium, it says as much about you as it does about them. They're playing down to their competition.

Miraculously, kids manage to take the most pathetic hiding spots in the world and make them worse. Rather than staying put, children jump out after a few seconds to check if anyone is about to find them. If there isn't someone nearby, kids shout to attract attention. Common phrases they yell include, "You can't find me," "I'm over here," "Are you even looking?" and "Stop taking a nap." Like everyone else born since 1980, your children have short attention spans and a burning desire to be the center of attention. Neither is a great quality to have in a time when discretion can be the difference between life and death. "Millennial" is just a euphemism for "zombie bait."

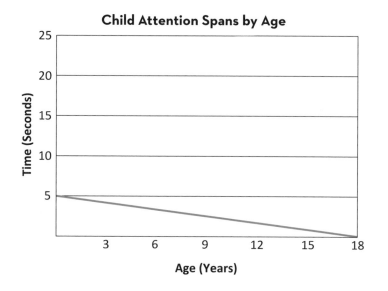

HIDDEN POTENTIAL

The only way your children will make it through the zombie apocalypse is if you teach them how to hide. This isn't a skill they can learn from a teacher or coach. Those people will already be dead. You'll be the ideal mentor by default. Don't hide from this responsibility. It would be an ironic demonstration of your skills, but subtlety is wasted on children.

The first step to making your kids better at hiding is to be honest with them. I've advocated lying over and over in this book, but this is one situation where telling the truth is the best approach. The faster you tear them down, the faster you can tear them down some more. Rebuilding them would make them more confident, but you really want their first instinct to be to cower.

Send your children off to hide on their own. Then tell them how much their hiding places suck. Explain in excruciating detail how they let you down both as your children and as human beings. Use hand motions and maybe a few graphs or charts. The sooner your kids stop feeling good about their evasion skills, the sooner they'll have a shot at survival. Self-esteem is for species that aren't on the verge of extinction. Just be careful with your timing. Only make your kids cry when there are no zombies around. Kids seldom learn valuable life lessons when they're dead.

After your children understand how bad they are at hiding on their own, they'll be ready for your expert guidance. This is your chance to shine as a parent. Challenge them to games of hide and seek. These vital life-and-death training sessions will look suspiciously like spending quality time with your kids. Work the illusion to your advantage. If they think you care about them, they're less likely to shrug off all your advice. Studies show well-loved children only ignore 75 percent of what they're told. You're guaranteed to teach them something if you repeat yourself at least four times. Since you're a parent, that should come naturally.

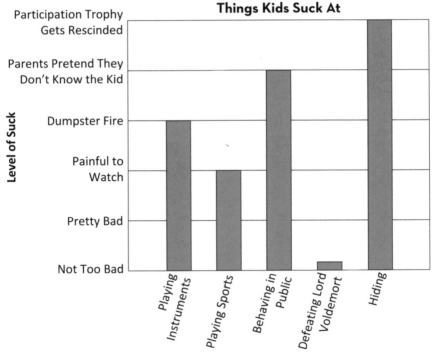

Now these can't be ordinary games of hide and seek. To simulate the pressures of a real-life zombie encounter, add penalties and rewards. Set a time limit. If your children hide for the full duration without being found, offer them some of the looted candy in your secret stash. If your children ask why you have a secret stash, calmly explain to them that they're a ravenous horde of locusts that devours everything good in your life. They'll understand. Don't just hand the candy over, though. If they win, be sure to taste-test the prizes yourself first. You know, for safety reasons.

If your children lose the hide and seek challenge, make the penalty proportionately awful. If a zombie found them, it would bite them on the spot. You shouldn't go that far. It might make your kids think you've already turned. After all the time you'll have spent berating them as part of these hiding lessons, it'll be a bad idea to give them a pretext to kill you.

The best penalties discourage a certain behavior while also benefiting the family. If you find your kids before time expires, make them do an unbearable chore like cleaning the bathrooms or listening to you talk about your childhood. Emphasize the part where kids today have it easy compared to the kids of your generation, even though you grew up in the era before zombies. You also grew up before the internet, which your children enjoyed for years before the world ended. It evens out. The more painful this story is for your kids, the stronger their incentive to hide better next time. But try not to literally bore them to death. Make the zombies work for it.

The time limit for the game should be exceptionally long. Since zombies don't have anywhere better to be, they could linger outside a hiding spot for hours or even days. Tell your kids to hunker down and stay there indefinitely. You'll let them know when time expires. It'll teach them to be patient. It'll also give you some peace and quiet for once in your life. Feel free to play this "game" for hours a day. Your sanity will thank you.

SIZE MATTERS

Older kids are better at hiding, but there are fewer places for them to disappear. It's one of the many drawbacks of growing up. You'll counteract some of those negatives by accident. A lack of food should keep your kids short. Combine that with children's natural jellyfish-like bone structure and your kids should be able to squeeze into seemingly impossible spots where zombies will never find them well into their preteen years. Your kids will be grateful you failed them as a provider every time they shimmy into a new, tiny hideout. Although there might be some lingering resentment if they hoped to make it in the NBA.

The Best Hiding Spots for Kids

Hiding Spot	Pro	Con
In a Deep Freezer	Large, dark, and mostly soundproof.	Kids will smell like rotten food for the rest of the apocalypse.
In the Dirty Clothes Hamper	Will mask their scent.	In an era without working washing machines, the odor might cause lasting brain damage.
Inside the Dryer	No electricity means a sibling can't turn it on.	It's fairly soundproof. You could lose a kid inside for days.
In the Bathtub	Great way to trick your kid into taking a bath.	No escape options. Doubles as a zombie feeding trough.
Under the Bed	Dark and low to the ground.	Without vacuums to keep them in check, dust bunnies will grow bold and deadly.
Pantry	Dark and hidden.	Kids will eat all the food.

Crawlspace	Hard for zombies to gain access.	Spiders. You're better off with the zombies.
In the Closet	Puts a door between your kids and any zombies.	To fit in your kids, you'll have to clean it.
Tree House	High above zombies.	You'll have to build it. There goes your weekend.

THE PERFECT SPOT

That subheading is a lie. There is no perfect hiding spot. The best place to find cover will depend on where you are, who you're with, and what is chasing you. Use your best judgment, unless you're anything like me. Then you should use your spouse's best judgment.

Still, as long as you stay calm, you can bravely cower somewhere until the zombies go away. And if they refuse to leave, well, you can always run or fight. Be sure to finish the chapters on those topics before you make your decision. If you're stuck in a hiding spot right now, this is the perfect time to browse through them. It turns out all it took to make people read again was the end of the world.

But if you're not in stealth mode yet, follow these tips to get ready in advance. It might save your life or, even better, save you from getting yelled at by your spouse.

✓ **Do** dress your kids in appropriate footwear. Hiding can turn into running at a moment's notice. There's nothing worse than having to fight off zombies while you're still looking for the other shoe.

✗ **Don't** pick an uncomfortable spot. Whining will get you eaten. Bring extra pillows.

✓ **Do** wear colors that will blend in. Even a mindless zombie will notice a bright orange shirt in the middle of the woods. Your horrible fashion choices will finally catch up with you.

✗ **Don't** forget kids grow. A kitchen cabinet is a great hiding place when your child is four but not when they're sixteen. Either pick new hiding spots or train your child to be a contortionist.

✓ **Do** take a bottle or whatever else you need for hidden bathroom breaks. Don't pee freely, especially if you're hiding in a laundry pile.

✗ **Don't** expect a short stay. Zombies don't have any pressing engagements on their social calendars. They're still more popular than you.

✓ **Do** pack snacks. A growling stomach will give away your position. Also, hiding is super boring, and the best thing to do when bored is eat.

CHANGE OF PLAN

If you're too unmotivated to run away and too impatient to hide, fighting might be your best option. I'd tell you to read on to the next chapter, but you're probably also too lazy and impatient to finish an entire book. Props for making it this far, I guess. For the rest of you, read on even if you don't feel like killing zombies. As parents, you always need a plan C—and probably D through Q as well. I'm only giving you three plans. I'm a dad, not a machine.

CHAPTER 7

PACIFY THIS

When you can't run and you can't hide, there's only one option left: Fight. Well, I suppose you could give up and die, but that's hardly ideal. Your spouse and kids would be super mad at you. No one likes a quitter.

No matter how much of a pacifist you think you are, you have at least some skill at fighting. It's in your DNA. If there's one thing the human race is good at, it's killing. *Homo sapiens* invented murder before they invented language. When Cain killed Abel, there wasn't even a word for it yet. The ancient Hebrews eventually settled on "pwned." Zombies should think twice before they mess with us. Too bad they don't have enough brainpower to think even once.

Parents with small children are especially good in a fight. It's only natural. Every time a hiker gets mauled by a bear, it's because the bear was defending its cubs. Protecting offspring makes animals act with supernatural aggression and strength. Basically nature found a way to take normal bears and make them even deadlier. It's amazing they haven't conquered the earth. And the only thing scarier than a mama bear is a mama human. They can kill with a single icy stare. I should know. My wife stopped my heart twice the last time I forgot to take out the trash.

Parents will need every ounce of that primal adrenaline once civilization collapses. Zombies are a tougher foe than bears. Grizzlies can feel fear and pain, but the undead know only hunger. Plus, when you die, you don't turn into a bear. That would be awesome. For the record, if I had to choose how the world would end, the bear apocalypse would be a much better way to go. I wouldn't mind my loved ones dying if they all came back as pandas.

SMASHING GOOD TIME

While the only way to kill a zombie is to destroy its brain, there is no shortage of ways to get that done. Through thousands of years of trial and error, humans have tested every killing method possible—and impossible. No army could take itself seriously if it didn't have at least one shrink ray on the drawing board—or on a tiny scrap of paper, if the ray worked. Even the simple act of punching a man in the face is covered in slightly different ways by hundreds of competing hand-to-hand combat systems. No other field has received such in-depth study, and for good reason. Reading a book will never be as fulfilling as karate-chopping someone in the face.

There's nothing I can say in this modest book to compete with the collective battle wisdom of the human race, so I won't try. Instead, this chapter focuses on the unique ways parents can kill zombies that childless people would never think of. For inspiration, look no further than your own kids. To be a child is to be at war. Whether it's a soft cuddly toy or a bike with fancy handlebar tassels, to a kid, everything is a weapon. Parents have been discouraging that behavior for centuries. Now we must act like our own violent sons and daughters if we want to survive. Finding your inner child means turning into an unstoppable killing machine.

WAKE-UP CALL

To fight effectively, you must be alert at all times. Zombies are most likely to catch you when you're tired or distracted. As a mom or dad, you already feel that way 100 percent of the time. True parents can fall asleep anywhere at any time. But with the added exhaustion of the apocalypse thrown in, no matter how long you nod off, you'll never feel well-rested. Caffeine is only a temporary solution. The world's supply will run out quickly, leaving those who depend on it withdrawn and homicidal. To avoid both killing and being killed during the inevitable caffeine crash, you'll need to do something else to stay alert. And that thing is panic.

Other guides tell you to stay calm. They couldn't be more wrong. Panic is good. It floods your entire body with raw, uncut adrenaline, preparing you to fight or flee without a second of hesitation. To survive in a world full of zombies, you'll need to do a lot of both. Panic allows you to make quick, irrational decisions in moments of crisis, when slow, methodical logic would get you killed. It's better to be quickly wrong than slowly right. The ability to act hastily without regard for what happens next is what separates us from zombies. It's a founding principle of America.

Panic will make you alert to the point of paranoia and fill your arms and legs with the flailing, undirected strength of a drowning swimmer, at least temporarily. You'll be able to randomly thrash your way through any zombie horde. Having your kids nearby will help. If there's a legitimate threat to your offspring, your body will automatically pump all of its adrenaline into your system. There won't be many dating options once the majority of the earth's population is wiped out. Your chances of starting a second family are exactly zero. Your body will give you everything you need to fight off zombies and ensure the survival of the progeny you already have. It's your job to use this surge in one frantic burst before it runs out. Panic wisely.

For most parents, panicking comes naturally. If it doesn't for you, here are a few dos and don'ts to keep in mind:

✖ **Don't** calm down. A short-lived panic attack is almost as useless as no panic attack at all.

✓ **Do** make your kids panic, too. Tell them about your long odds of survival. Soon their bodies will be pumping out emergency hormones as well. Together, you'll be unstoppable.

✖ **Don't** panic too early. Freaking out is exhausting. If you do it when it isn't necessary for your survival, you'll be too tired to do it when you really need it.

✓ **Do** hyperventilate. Suck down air like the earth is running out. It'll super-oxygenate your blood and prep you for feats of amazing speed and strength. It's what pro athletes do.

✖ **Don't** be ashamed. Other parents might look down on you for being afraid. Soon they'll be dead, and you'll be killing the walking corpses they leave behind.

- ✓ **Do** give it your all. Panic is an all-or-nothing situation. There's no sense in saving up for a future panic. If you don't do it right this time, there won't be a next one.

- ✗ **Don't** get loud. If you make too much noise, you'll attract zombies. A quiet panic is an effective panic.

- ✓ **Do** lose control. You'll only reach your true potential if you're motivated by unmitigated terror. If you're still using your brain, you're doing it wrong.

EVEN THE ODDS

Once you've hyper-accelerated your heart rate with a healthy level of fear, it's time to act. Your first duty in any zombie attack is to tilt the numbers in your favor. You do this on a daily basis without even thinking about it. Your kids come at you in groups and try to overwhelm you with sheer volume. A pack of children can ask a million questions per minute. This is not hyperbole. I've counted. Their hope is as you say "yes" to "Can I go the bathroom?" and "Do I have to wash my hands?" you might accidentally slip in an affirmative response to "Can we go to Disneyland?" or "Can I play with lighter fluid?" Hopefully those last two questions are unrelated. Mickey Mouse isn't shy about suing.

To deal with children, you have to spread them out. Send kids to different rooms to complete pointless tasks. That potted cactus doesn't need someone to read it poetry, but your kids don't know that. Once you've pulled this off, your children will be scattered enough for you to deal with them one by one, breaking their wills as you go. A happy child is a defiant child. Make them feel the existential angst that fills the pit of your stomach every second of your waking life. Then they'll be too depressed to cause trouble.

Dealing with zombie hordes in confined spaces works on the same principle. Your goal is to spread them out so you can take them down individually. If you're at home, tactically withdraw deeper into your dwelling, dodging through doorways and over obstacles that will cause zombies to stumble and drift apart. If you have kids, your house will already be one big obstacle course, even if you try desperately to keep it clean. Zombie or not, anyone would be lucky to make it through that in one piece.

To further split up the zombies, find the loudest, most annoying toy your kids own. In my house, it's a large stuffed bumblebee that talks to itself at random hours of the night. I don't care what the manufacturer's tag says—that thing was made by Satan. In a zombie combat scenario, throw the toy one way and move the other. With luck, some or all of the zombies will head off to chase after it. Kill any that follow you, then take out the distracted ones from behind. This is a dirty, underhanded tactic. Congratulations, you finally have what it takes to survive.

THE FAMILY THAT FIGHTS TOGETHER, STAYS TOGETHER

Work your kids into zombie combat as best you can. A rotting zombie skull has the same breaking point as the rind of a watermelon, a conclusion I base on absolutely nothing. One of the many downsides of the pre-apocalypse world is it's hard to find zombie skulls for testing purposes. Without the real thing, you'll have to get creative when assessing your children's skills. Before the world ends, buy as many watermelons as you can and set them up for a demonstration. Let your kids take a crack at them with their fists, feet, bats, and whatever else you think might be around when the zombies show up. If your kids destroy the watermelon to your satisfaction, let them help you in battle. If they don't, well, at least you can still eat the watermelon.

Children who are too small to help will need to be shoved aside and protected when the real combat starts. But if you're cornered to the point where you have to fight, your kids won't be able to stay out of the way. You'll have to step over or around them the entire time. This should feel familiar. You've been doing it since the moment they first became mobile. Zombies, however, aren't limber enough to dodge your children and will likely fall over. This adds another complication you don't need. A zombie at ankle level is as deadly as one standing up. Do your best to stomp their heads before they can bite your children's feet. This is one time when tall footwear will come in handy. I knew there was a reason every woman in America started wearing riding boots.

Use the unreliability of your children to your advantage. If you're trapped in a room with your kids and there are zombies outside the door, tell your children to be completely silent. They'll immediately be as quiet as an erupting volcano. When the noise becomes deafening, stand to the side of the door and crack it open a little. The zombies will burst in and head straight for your kids. Kill the zombies from behind. Keep in mind it's hard to estimate zombie numbers through a closed door. Hopefully the swarm will be manageable. I cannot stress enough how much trouble you'll be in with your spouse if your kids die while you use them as bait.

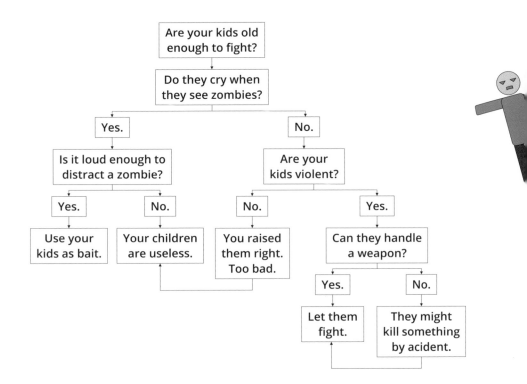

BATTER UP

If you're like most parents, you've spent thousands of dollars equipping your children for sports they've either already abandoned or will as soon as they discover video games and recreational drugs. All that gear gathering dust in your garage will have a new purpose once the world ends. Pads designed to stop sports injuries can also prevent zombie bites. Football and hockey gear will be especially useful. They encase kids in a hard plastic shell that rotting teeth can't penetrate. The only problem is they also limit kids' mobility and provide a lot more surface area for zombies to latch onto. In the zombie apocalypse, there are no penalties for holding.

Athletic helmets are as effective on offense as defense. The best way to destroy zombie brains is with the sport that already destroys brains all the time. Put your kids in their peewee football helmets. Then blow a whistle and let them charge. The goal is a helmet-to-zombie-skull collision. If your kids are too short, they can still hit a zombie in the midsection and knock it over. Then they should stomp it with their cleats. Again, this isn't an unknown phenomenon on the football field, so it should come naturally to your kids. If it bothers them, tell them to imagine they're stomping grapes. The only difference is instead of a delicious wine, you'll end up with a gory mess on your kitchen floor. Stock up on paper towels.

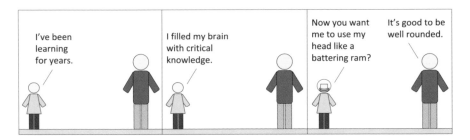

If you prefer your kids to keep a bit of distance between themselves and the zombies, youth sports provide a variety of reach weapons. Baseball bats will let your kids thwack zombies from a few feet away. Metal bats have the most damage potential, but you can give your kids the wooden kind if they want to imitate their favorite players in the major leagues. The end of the world is no reason to stop having role models. If your kids have bad aim, give them softball bats, which are much wider than their baseball counterparts. The only way to miss with a softball bat is not to swing at all. Don't be surprised if your kids still strike out.

The sports weapons available to you will vary by region. In Canada, every child is born holding a hockey stick. It's a wonder their mothers survive labor. On the east coast of the U.S., you can't move up a tax bracket until your kid plays lacrosse. In the U.K., you're not legally an adult until you own more than one cricket bat. For my American readers, cricket is a sport that involves hitting a ball, not smashing crickets with a stick—at least according to this angry correction note from my editor. This book now contains one real fact. It's officially educational.

Be aware, however, that if you let your kids use any of these weapons in your house, they'll destroy everything you own. This will happen whether or not there are zombies. For veteran parents, this won't be a problem. Only rookies still own nice things.

TOY CHEST/WEAPONS LOCKER

Not every family is full of burned-out child athletes. Some kids never do sports at all. Maybe they realize the futility of training for thousands of hours at a skill they will never use in the real world. Or maybe their bodies finally melded to the couch. Whatever the reason, not everyone has a used sporting goods store sitting around in their attic. Fear not. Your kids still own plenty of other objects that can kill or maim. Just check the warning labels.

Most toys spell out in huge, scary letters how they can kill. That makes them easy to weaponize. If the warning says "don't," do. While all toys can maim children, only certain types can destroy zombies. Choking hazards won't do any good against the undead. If a zombie swallows one, it can still bite, infect, and kill you. Don't get bitten by zombies. Or by anyone, for that matter. That's a good rule to live by, even when there's no apocalypse.

The best toys to weaponize require safety goggles. Zombies see. They have eyeballs, and they use them. You have a house full of children's play-things that twirl, spark, shoot projectiles, and inevitably end up in some-one's eye. It's time to use that to your advantage. If a zombie corners your kids, tell your children to grab the most dangerous toys they can find and aim for the zombie's face. A spinning fairy wing or flying foam dart could permanently lacerate a zombie's corneas. A blinded zombie could still track you and your children by smell, but everything in your house will uniformly stink. The only thing that will run out faster than food in the apocalypse is air fresheners.

Toys that can be customized into stabbing implements are the deadliest of all. Any plaything made of hard plastic can be sharpened into a shiv. It doesn't sound like a good zombie weapon, but never underestimate the stab-bing power of a sharpened Barbie. A shiv will punch through a zombie skull like, well, a shiv through a zombie skull. It's not a well-known idiom now, but I'm sure it'll replace "like a hot knife through butter" in years to come.

Even playthings that only look dangerous can be useful. Encourage your kids to play with toy guns. In better times, you might have worried they could be mistaken for real guns and get your kids into trouble. In the zombie apocalypse, that's exactly what you want to happen. Zombies won't be frightened by armed children, but other survivors might be. Quite frankly, if you see a strange toddler holding a gun-shaped object, you should get the hell out of there, no questions asked. Other humans who think your kids are packing heat are less likely to kill your family and take your stuff. The worst those strangers will do to you is judge your parenting skills. Let them. They'll be too busy being self-righteous to hear the zombies shuffling up behind them.

BOARD GAME NIGHT

Having the right tools to kill zombies won't be enough. Your kids also must have the right attitude. Children endlessly fight their own siblings, but when it comes to zombies, many kids will be reluctant to engage. The fastest way to bolster their fighting spirit is with board games. If you suspect a zombie attack is imminent, sit down with your kids and play Monopoly. By the end, everyone will be ready to kill each other. Channel that anger toward the undead. Then sit back and watch proudly as your kids destroy an entire zombie horde.

Other games can help your kids fight as well. Twister will limber them up for the physical demands of combat; Battleship will attune them to the cat-and-mouse nature of avoiding zombies; and Chutes and Ladders will remind them life is random, unfair, and pointless, so they might as well cheat. After enough time with these games, your kids will become agile, cunning, and indifferent to whether they live or die. They will be terrible human beings but perfect zombie slayers. It's every parent's dream.

FIGHT OR FLIGHT

As a parent, you're an expert at avoiding confrontation. Not every battle is worth fighting. Sometimes it's easier to hide in the closet and cry. No wonder the walk-in ones are so popular. But in the zombie apocalypse, as with the rest of life, there are some situations where a fight can't be avoided. If you must fight, fight to win. Or at least go for a respectable draw. Or a loss where you can still sneak away at the end somehow. Basically, don't die. And don't let your kids die, either. It doesn't matter how bad you are at panicking at the right time or fighting with Barbie shivs as long as you get the right results. You succeed as a parent as long as your kids live to whine another day.

CHAPTER 8

STROLLING FOR TROUBLE

Parents have many weapons at their disposal, but only one has the power to destroy anyone or anything in its path. A soldier has a rifle. A Jedi has a lightsaber. A parent has an umbrella stroller.

Make no mistake: This is a weapon disguised as transportation. If you have a child young enough to ride in one, consider yourself lucky. You'll always be armed and ready to defend your family. I feel bad for parents whose kids are too old. You can't push an empty umbrella stroller before the world ends. People will wonder if you're missing a child or looking to kidnap one. You can't stay on the lookout for zombies if you're running from the police.

Umbrella Stroller
Height: 42 in.
Weight: 9 lbs.
Top Speed: 6 mph
Destructive power:
Wrath of God

An umbrella stroller is lightweight and folds up at a moment's notice, at least in theory. In the open position, you can use it like a battering ram to trip zombies. Closed, you can pick it up and swing it like a club. Its hollow metal rods give it the right balance of strength and speed to strike a crushing blow against any opponent. And the best part is it's entirely unregulated. Unlike guns, flamethrowers, and combat aircraft, there are no laws restricting umbrella stroller ownership. You could go out tonight and buy fifty of them without a background check. Of course, no sane person needs that many. Also, it wouldn't be fair. Save some zombie killing for the rest of us.

Weapons and Their Waiting Periods

Banned No Matter How Long You Wait	Short Waiting Period	No Waiting Period
Hand grenades, nuclear weapons, aircraft carriers, lightsabers.	Most handguns and semi-automatic rifles.	Umbrella strollers, any booby trap featured in the movie *Home Alone*.

I didn't invent using a child transportation device as a combat weapon. Umbrella stroller fencing is a gentleman's sport that dates back more than a century. Sure, it's not in the Olympics, but only because snobbish traditionalists are afraid it will overshadow classic events like swimming or dressage. After you've seen two skilled stroller fencers do battle, it's hard to get excited about a dancing horse.

The development of stroller fighting was inevitable. If something exists, humans will use it as a weapon. That's the most basic law of physical matter. When England debuted the first giant prams, parents immediately tested them against each other in demolition derbies. The children were still inside them, which explains the high child mortality rate back then. In today's more enlightened times, direct baby-on-baby collisions are discouraged, but bored parents still find ways to duel. Look at the metal bars on any stroller.

If they have mysterious dings and scrapes, a mom or dad definitely picked it up and swung it like a broadsword. And now you understand why parents only hang out with other parents.

The deadliness of the umbrella stroller is beyond dispute, but there are still a few naysayers out there. "If strollers are so dangerous," they say to themselves because they have no friends, "why haven't there been any stroller murders in recorded history?" First of all, stroller murder records only go back to the mid-1960s. I assume the period before that was a real bloodbath.

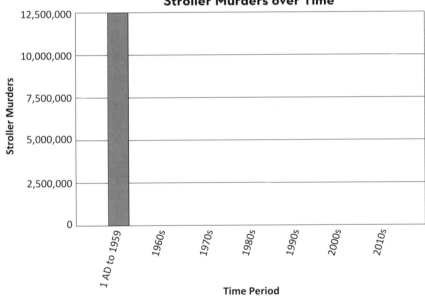

Second, strollers are way more effective against the undead than they are against the living. There's a highly scientific explanation for why, but the short answer is that dumb, slow zombies are easier to thump on the head. As if that weren't convincing enough, I'll now prove it to you with some completely fictional scenarios I made up off the top of my head.

TOTALLY PLAUSIBLE STROLLER COMBAT SCENARIO 1

You and your family are out for a walk. You push a baby in a stroller while a few bigger kids walk, or more accurately drag their feet until they fall behind and then sprint ahead for absolutely no reason. You thought this would be a simple two-block stroll, but now it's turned into a three-mile death march. You're tired, irritable, and cursing this stupid fad of going places with the power of your own two feet. That's when you spot it: a zombie shambling toward you. Never fear. You're already pushing the greatest zombie-slaying weapon ever invented. I still don't understand why they sell it in the baby aisle.

The first thing to do is clear the combat zone. In other situations, your spouse and kids might be able to help. But you're pushing a weapon of mass destruction. The last thing you want to do is wipe out your family as collateral damage.

That's not to say the rest of your family will leave willingly. Ditching them will require subtlety and tact. Unfortunately, as a parent, you have neither. Yelling at tiny humans all day to stop eating sand and licking each other tends to make you blunt. But if you tell your family there's a zombie, that will only make them more likely to stay, either to see the monster firsthand or—if it's the first one you've ever encountered—to mock you for being crazy. When you take the baby out of the stroller and hand them off to a family member, your spouse will be even more likely to stick around. Getting ready for a zombie fight looks a lot like abandoning your family so you can start over somewhere new. Don't get any ideas. Instead, calmly neutralize your spouse's sudden clinginess by being yourself. If you're like me, you've been driving people away your entire life. You've got this.

Since zombies are slower than humans, your family should be able to calmly turn around and walk away from danger. That's the theory. In practice, executing even the simplest maneuver with kids is virtually impossible. They naturally do the opposite of what you tell them, unless they anticipated you'd use reverse psychology. Then they do the opposite of whatever you said. If you understood those sentences at all, you've already spent too much time with your children.

Once your spouse and kids turn around to leave, it's your job to act as a rear guard as they escape—or as they stop ten feet away and bicker about something pointless while you risk your life for their safety. At this point, you might be tempted to deal with the zombie with your bare hands. Like almost everything else in your life, this is a bad idea. That emaciated corpse could be stronger than you. Let's be honest: Kids weren't the first excuse you used to skip the gym. Plus the flesh on the zombie's forearm could tear off when you grab it, allowing the zombie to slip forward and attack you. That would be deadly and more than a little gross. Always carry hand sanitizer.

Now that you've lost all confidence in your hand-to-hand fighting skills, you're ready to unleash the fury of the umbrella stroller. The first technique is a rolling frontal assault. It's the easiest and laziest of attacks. It's the sweatpants of combat.

Rolling Stroller Attack:

1. Verify the baby is no longer in the stroller. If you forgot to hand the kid to your spouse, this won't end well.
2. Aim for one of the zombie's shins.
3. Charge forward with the stroller.
4. As the zombie falls, yell a dad joke. Be creative. "Timber!" and "Help, I've fallen and I can't get up" are already taken.

Note that zombie battles don't end just because you make contact and utter a witty one-liner. The undead are immune to all burns, both physical and emotional. If the zombie is walking toward you when you take out one leg, it could fall forward. If this happens, sidestep and keep the stroller between yourself and the zombie. You'll need quick reflexes to pull it off, so there's a good chance this is the point where you'll die. Sorry if your life was short and pointless. At least you lived long enough to buy my book.

If, when the zombie falls, it doesn't land on you, it'll reach out for your legs. Make sure it grabs the stroller instead. The zombie will become tangled up with it, buying you time to escape. This is only effective if your spouse won't mind losing the stroller and you're okay carrying your baby for the rest of the apocalypse. If you have strong arms, that's not a big deal. But I have little upper body strength and a wife who frowns on me losing our personal property, so this method won't work for me. If you want to kill the zombie and also stay married, you'll find the solution you need in scenario two.

TOTALLY PLAUSIBLE STROLLER COMBAT SCENARIO 2

This time, let's say you're pushing an umbrella stroller by yourself. Your baby is safely buckled in the seat. Then a zombie approaches. You need the stroller for battle, but your child is selfishly using it. What should you do? I recommend the tried-and-true tactic known as the baby toss. Setting the baby on the ground won't get the child far enough away from the combat zone. This is especially true if the child can walk or crawl. As we saw previously, kids are naturally drawn toward anything that can kill them. You have to get the baby far enough away that it will take them at least a few moments to get back. That's why the baby must be tossed, not set on the ground. It's science.

The key word here is "toss," not "throw." The goal is a gentle landing with little velocity. Do not throw overhand. Babies are surprisingly un-aerodynamic. You'll never get the tight spiral you want, and it'll be a rough landing. Not to mention babies are heavy. A child as young as one can weigh as much as twenty footballs. Even an NFL quarterback would struggle to hit a receiver with that. The best anyone could hope for overhand with a baby would be a shot-put–style toss, which wouldn't get the job done either. It would start with lots of loft and end with a sudden stop. Expect lots of crying, even if the kid sticks the landing. Babies are never happy.

| Wrong: Baby Hail Mary | Wrong: Baby Field Goal | Wrong: Baby Fast-Pitch Softball |

Author's Note: Real babies might not have visible velocity lines. Results may vary.

A two-handed underhand throw is the way to go. It won't impress any spectators, but you can regain their respect by totally beating the crap out of the zombie once your kid is in the clear. Take both of your hands and put one firmly on each side of the child's waist. Pull back a short distance, then toss the child off the sidewalk. Be sure to follow through with your arms. The last thing you want is for your child to fall short and land on the sidewalk with you. Such a weak toss would result in injuries to the child and the forfeiture of your man card. Or woman card. Shame knows no gender lines. Aim for the cleanest landing spot possible. If you and the kid both survive the zombie attack, you'll have to answer for any stains on the baby's clothes when you get home.

With the kid safely out of the way for twenty or thirty seconds, it's time for the club approach.

Swinging the Umbrella Stroller Like a Club

1. Calmly fold up the stroller.
2. If it's still not folded up, try a little less calmly.
3. Seriously, what engineer thought this design was a good idea? Try swearing. That usually helps.
4. Okay, it's folded up now. Did the zombie eat you yet? No? Good.
5. Hold the stroller above your head like a bludgeon.

6. Utter a memorable sword-based catchphrase, like "By the power of Grayskull!" or "It's over, Anakin, I have the high ground!" I know a club and a sword are completely different, but the pool of memorable club sayings is disappointingly shallow.
7. Swing the stroller like a club at the side of the zombie's head.
8. Wait for the zombie to fall over.
9. Retrieve your child. Hopefully they're still there.

That last step is critical. You'll look like an idiot if you topple one zombie only for another zombie to then walk up and eat your kid. The undead seldom fight fair, and they never feel bad about it. They're the New England Patriots of monsters.

Be sure to practice these maneuvers in advance. Folding up an umbrella stroller is notoriously tricky even without an approaching zombie. Once the stroller locks in the open position, it's entirely possible it will never fold up again. That's my experience, though my wife has never had any problem whatsoever. Apparently, I need to pull or push or perform a voodoo hex. Whatever the last step is, I miss it every single time. I'm positive I'm not the only incompetent parent out there. In short, if you're an adult with reasonable hand-eye coordination and functioning opposable thumbs, you will be fine folding up the stroller and using it like a blunt force weapon. But if you're anything like me, you'll be better off admitting defeat and following the tactics I describe in scenario three.

TOTALLY PLAUSIBLE STROLLER COMBAT SCENARIO 3

It's the same situation as last time. You're alone with a baby, a stroller, and a zombie. You've successfully completed the baby toss. Now for an approach that should work for parents who couldn't use the methods in the first two scenarios. If you can't pull off this one, either, maybe child rearing isn't for you. Consider other pursuits like horticulture or stamp collecting.

Four-Point Battering Ram Stroller Attack

1. Grab the still-opened stroller off the ground by both handles.
2. Point the stroller directly at the zombie.
3. Charge forward.
4. Make contact squarely in the middle of the zombie's chest.
5. Watch as the zombie topples backward.
6. Wipe any zombie guts off the wheels so you don't leave a trail back to your house.

This is what umbrella strollers were built for. Moving children was an unintended side effect.

Using the stroller as a battering ram is safer than employing the rolling shin attack, which could trip the zombie forward, or the swinging club approach, which would knock the zombie to the side. With the zombie on its back, you'll have extra moments to get away. With any luck, the zombie will be comfortable down there and take a nap. Zombies don't sleep, but there's a first time for everything. The zombie also might break its head open on the sidewalk. A concrete slab almost gave me a concussion once. It's about time artificial rock fought for the good guys.

A popular variation on this attack is to pick up the stroller and charge forward like before, but aim for a standing zombie's head rather than its chest. Once you stick its head between the wheels, the zombie will be braced there as it keeps moving forward. You can then use the stroller to steer the zombie in one direction or the other. If there's a busy street next to you, this could remove the zombie from the picture permanently. Just make sure it's not a living neighbor having a bad day. I don't want to be liable for inciting any stroller murders.

THE FULL ARSENAL

Those were just a few of the dozens of different umbrella stroller combat techniques that will be available to parents in the zombie apocalypse. I wanted to write an entire book on stroller fencing, but the world isn't ready for that much useful information in one place. I guess someone else will have to win the Nobel Prize in literature. In the meantime, here's a quick rundown of other stroller moves that could save your life. Feel free to practice them in front of a mirror over and over again until you get them right. That won't freak out your spouse at all.

Other Stroller Attacks

Name	Description
The Whirlwind	Use the hooked handles of a stroller to catch a zombie by the neck. Spin in circles until one of you falls down. Try not to throw up.
Lance Attack	Fold up the stroller, place it under your arm, and charge ahead at full speed like you're jousting. Then offer a rose to the nearest damsel.
Figure Skater Special	Swing the stroller like a club, but aim for the kneecaps.
Drive-by	Get a running start. Jump on the back of the stroller to glide by the zombie. Punch it in the face as you pass. Warning: The stroller may collapse under your weight if you're older than two.
Bait and Switch	Leave your kid in the stroller. When a zombie goes in for the kill, bull-rush them from a hiding place off to the side. Don't be late.

The Nutcracker	Collapse the stroller and swing it like a golf club at the zombie's nuts. The zombie won't feel anything, but it'll make you feel better.
Exit Stage Left	Use the hooks on the stroller handles to snag the zombie's feet and pull them out from under it. Tell it to break a leg.
Sacrifice Bunt	Hold a closed stroller horizontally in front of you like you're about to bunt a baseball. Run forward and knock over zombies. Die with honor.

ORDER NOW

Get your hands on an umbrella stroller before it's too late. After the zombie apocalypse starts, people will kill each other over them. Actually, the killing will only go one way since anyone who doesn't have one won't stand a chance against someone who does. Entire military units will drop their M4s in favor of umbrella strollers. If you already have one, pat yourself on the back. For perhaps the only time ever, having a kid paid off.

CHAPTER 9

THE HOME FRONT

There's no such thing as a child-proof home. The best you can hope for is a home-proof child. Over time, your kids will grow immune to all the daily dangers you overlooked. They'll develop tough skin from playing with knives and an unstoppable immune system thanks to a liberal interpretation of the five-second rule. Ironically, your failure to keep your children safe could save their lives—or drive them away the second they're tall enough to reach a doorknob. Only time will tell.

Hopefully they'll stay home. Your house is the most secure place to be in the zombie apocalypse. In fact, your kids will be safer in your home after the world ends than they were before. Electrical outlets and stove burners will be harmless playthings once the power and natural gas cut out. There won't be anything left in the house to harm your children besides splinters. So forget elaborate survival bunkers and abandoned nuclear silos. Your own home is the perfect place to ride out the apocalypse. Just throw a rug over the hardwood floors first.

Your house isn't that far from being zombie-ready right now. Contrary to what home-buying couples on TV might say, your home does not need a total gut-job. It also doesn't need granite countertops, stainless steel appliances, or space for entertaining. It's hard to impress your friends when everyone is dead. From that point forward, the only people who will see the inside of your humble dwelling will be your own family and any looters or zombies who smash their way in. There won't be any pressure to keep up appearances. The zombie apocalypse will be a great time to be a homemaker.

Decorations That Will Be Pointless in the Zombie Apocalypse

Decoration	Why It's Pointless
Throw Pillows	Nobody knows what these do in the normal world. In the apocalypse, they'll just make your house more flammable. Throw them away.
Accent Walls	All colors look the same in dim candlelight.
Crown Molding	You can't watch for zombies if you're staring at ceiling joints.
Hardwood Floors	Louder than carpet. The zombies that hear you sneaking around won't care that it's real bamboo.
Quartz Countertops	Won't make that canned corn any less expired.

| Glass Shower Doors | Eliminate any chance of hiding from zombies in the shower. |
| Gas Fireplace | Natural gas will run out. Good luck lighting fake ceramic logs. |

Your home will need only a few minor modifications once your nice, quiet neighborhood becomes an undead hellscape. Every zombie survival guide explains how to turn your house into an impregnable fortress with boarded-up windows and a single passageway in and out. For families, that's a death trap. People with kids can't wall themselves in. First of all, the smell would be unbearable. Children are small. You'd think their odors would be scaled proportionately, but the opposite is true. Children are covered in a layer of slime that absorbs every scent they've ever encountered. My oldest daughter still smells like a waffle joint I visited one time three years ago. We went through the drive-thru. Daily baths can't stop the smell, but they can mask it for a while. Even that won't be an option after the zombies show up. It's hard enough to get kids to clean up when the water is warm and welcoming. When the only bathing option left is a cold stream three miles away, that will be the end of bath night. Sealing yourself in a house with your kids will turn your home into an olfactory torture chamber. Open a window to maintain consciousness.

The second reason you shouldn't seal up your house is that with kids, you always need multiple escape options. You don't know which room they'll be in when zombies attack, but chances are it'll be whichever one is the most inconvenient at the time. If you're at the front of the house when a break-in occurs, expect your kids to be three rooms away in the kitchen making themselves cardboard and ketchup sandwiches. I'm sure those will sound much tastier once you're starving.

It will be too hard to round up all your kids and shepherd them out a single available exit. Other survival guides say it's easier to guard a sole point of entry. The flipside is if zombies break through it, your house will turn into a giant lunchbox. Besides, boarding up the windows is a major violation of the fire code—which doesn't sound like a big deal until there's a fire. You'll be in a house full of lit candles and stumbling, clumsy children chasing each other in dim light. Be sure to loot some fire extinguishers.

Boarded-up windows are also a visible sign to passing looters that they should stop and take a closer look. A protected home is a home with something worth protecting. A boarded-up window is a billboard to the world that says, "Please kill me and take my stuff." When you nail up those plywood boards, you put the final nail in your own coffin.

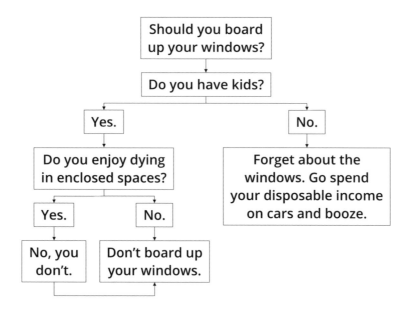

Don't despair yet. There are plenty of reasons to give up hope, but this isn't one of them. Instead of sealing up your windows with dead trees, cover them with blankets. The blankets will stop people and zombies from seeing into your house without preventing you from jumping out a window in an emergency or because you feel like it. Using a standard door can get old even for the best of us. Plus putting blankets over the windows will look trashy, and trashy houses never have anything worth looting. A passing scavenger will glance at your place and shudder. They're not looking for chewing tobacco or stock car commemorative plates. Their loss.

Whatever you do, don't keep the window coverings you already have. Normal curtains and blinds make homes seem well-kept and occupied, which is the opposite of what you're going for here. Besides, hanging normal window dressings is a nightmare. It's a great project to tackle with your spouse if you don't want to be married anymore. Blankets offer no such installation challenges. Hammer some nails through the blanket and into the top edge of the window sill and you'll have the right mix of privacy, survivability, and patheticness to throw off the zombie hordes and anyone else who is out to get you.

To maximize your home's lack of curb appeal, follow these pointers:

✓ **Do** use a thick blanket. There's no sense hanging up a transparent material. Windows already have one of those. It's called glass.

✗ **Don't** use a cool blanket. A brand new artificially distressed ironic retro pop culture comforter set will attract attention, not drive it away. Plus it probably costs as much as a mortgage payment. It isn't cheap pretending to be poor.

✓ **Do** cover every window, even the small, out-of-the-way ones that don't normally get much attention. That includes any bathroom windows. You'll need privacy while you do your most important work.

✗ **Don't** use a towel because it looks like a mini-blanket. It's completely different. Don't make me draw another diagram.

✔ **Do** use lots of nails. It's an easy project, and if you use them all up now, your spouse won't be able to make you build a deck.

✘ **Don't** ask anyone for help. It doesn't take a lot of brainpower to put a sharp, steel nail through a thin piece of cloth.

✔ **Do** nail up blankets at the very start of the zombie apocalypse. The wails of the dying outside your window should mask your hammer blows.

✘ **Don't** use a nail gun. It's too much fun. Your giddy screams of joy will get you eaten by nightfall.

OPEN DOOR POLICY

Modern homes come with thick metal security doors to keep out even the worst threat. Never lock them. This seems counterintuitive in a world where everything wants to kill you, but trust me on this. As a parent, the biggest threat to your safety is getting locked out of your own home. The last thing you want is to race back to your house with a pack of zombies in pursuit only to discover your baby dropped your keys three miles back. The only reason kids are fascinated with jingly objects is to create this exact scenario. It's their passive-aggressive way of getting back at you for not letting them eat dirt.

Sure, you could knock on your own front door, but any kids you left inside will take forever to answer. They never did anything quickly even in the best of times. By the time one of them opens the door, they'll find your partially eaten body and a pack of zombies who are ready for seconds. Even if the zombies don't catch you, there won't be any locksmiths left to replace the key. And if you do manage to find one, you can bet they'll overcharge. I'd rather die than be a sucker.

A locked door isn't a meaningful deterrent anyway. While it can delay you long enough for you to die on your own front steps, it won't keep out looters. In fact, it might draw their attention. If they test your front door and find out it's locked, they'll be curious as to what survival supplies you're hiding. If they can't break through the door, they'll smash a window. And all the glass surfaces on your house will only be protected by blankets. In hindsight, that seems like a bad idea. I wonder who told you to do it.

The truth is nothing will keep out a determined pursuer, dead or otherwise. If you had armor plating over all your doors and windows, a looter could simply burn down your house. Sure, they wouldn't get the supplies inside, but if they can't have it, no one can. It's easy to predict human actions once you assume everyone is a jerk. You'll be better off with windows that still open so you can easily escape rather than making a last stand in a house you only bought because it was in a good school district. The luster fades as soon as the first teacher tries to eat your kids.

As for zombies, they can't turn doorknobs, so an unlocked door will stop them as effectively as a locked one. You just have to make sure it's closed all the way so it latches. With kids in the house, this will be a challenge. It takes almost no effort to close a door all the way, but even that's asking too much. Children are in a hurry to get back to doing absolutely nothing. The only thing they respect less than you is your utility bill—or your firewood supply, once the power goes out. Don't bother sarcastically asking your kids if they're trying to heat the great outdoors. Kids are the primary cause of global warming.

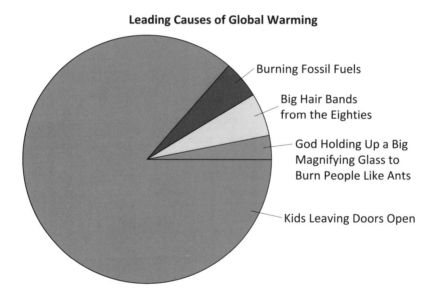

Leading Causes of Global Warming

Burning Fossil Fuels

Big Hair Bands from the Eighties

God Holding Up a Big Magnifying Glass to Burn People Like Ants

Kids Leaving Doors Open

INTO THE BREACH

Putting blankets over your windows and keeping the doors securely shut but unlocked is the closest you'll ever come to living in a stealth house. But in the unlikely event this gambit fails, you still have your best card left to play: your own child-ravaged home. Remember that your bad housekeeping is actually a powerful defensive measure. Stop aspiring to the perfect home and embrace the disaster. It's the only way you'll survive.

The first step is to give up on picking up around the house. It takes hours to clean a home but only seconds for children to destroy it. The floors of houses with kids are perpetually covered with plastic toys, dirty laundry, and random food bits from meals you may or may not have eaten this year. The only times homes with children are presentable is after hours of frantic cleaning before someone visits. Even then, your house only stays that way if you lock your kids in the basement.

Walking anywhere in a child-infested house is as dangerous as entering a coal mine. Keep it that way, at least on the first floor. I've mentioned before how hazardous this tactic is to zombies, but it's equally dangerous to human intruders. If looters break in, they'll slip and break their ankles on the hundreds of former birthday and Christmas gifts your kids just had to have but then immediately forgot about. If they push forward through the chaos, they'll never find anything worth stealing. Even you won't know where your good stuff is. Your most prized possessions will be buried under cheap plastic toys that take millions of years to decompose. They'll be safe for eternity. Any looter who sees that kind of desolation will give up and never come back. It's the perfect plan, other than the part where you'll still have to live there amidst the squalor.

Worst Toys to Step On

Toy	Consequence
Legos	If you're wearing shoes, you'll lose your footing. If you're not, you'll lose your foot.
Barbie Shoes	Sharper than steak knives.
Marbles	Aren't even a real game anymore. Only exist for tripping adults.
Plastic Army Men	Hurt like hell and make you feel unpatriotic for breaking them.
Matchbox Cars	You'll simultaneously break your ankle and ruin their collector's value.

The debris will have the same effect on zombies. Their balance is poor, and their bones are brittle. Unlike looters, however, zombies won't give up. If they think you're in the house, they'll keep going, no matter how suicidal the path ahead. Dying and rising again dulls their fear of death. Go figure.

Since zombies are stupid and relentless, you'll have to carefully position your random junk to stop them. First, leave all stringy toys right inside the front of the door. Jump ropes, Slinkys, and costume necklaces should all be piled there as inconveniently as possible. This will tangle up any zombies who pass through in the dark. This also works on humans. For parents with older kids, it's also a great way to enforce a curfew.

Next, make tall, teetering piles of boxes filled with books. They're heavy enough to crush anyone they fall on. "Light reading" is an oxymoron. A clumsy, flailing zombie will knock over those stacks, trapping itself underneath. Then you'll be free to kill it or leave it in place as a deterrent against looters and other unwanted living guests. Squirming piles of debris are great for scaring away salesmen.

All homes with kids in them drift toward chaos. The approach I described above just lets nature take its course. You're not a bad parent; you're an effective defensive strategist. Keep in mind this only applies to the first story. On the second floor, there's no excuse for living in a post-apocalyptic pigsty. That's why the laziest parents will ride out the end of the world in a single-story ranch. They'll never touch a dust pan again.

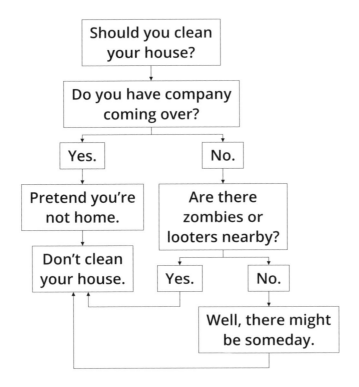

LANDSCAPE OF DOOM

If you're feeling ambitious, you can add traps outside your home as well. They'll have to be well disguised, though, or you'll ruin the whole uninhabited vibe you created with your window blankets. To avoid unwanted attention, any outdoor measures need to look like a haphazard eyesore, not a cohesive defensive grid. Basically, be bad at landscaping. Don't worry, if you have children, you can fail at anything.

The best way to disguise your outdoor traps is to make the outside of your house look like it's under construction. No one will bat an eye if you have dangerous scaffolding and building equipment outside your house for months or even years. As anyone who has ever renovated a home knows, if a contractor says something will take two months, the actual timeframe is forever. Those long-term renovations are extremely dangerous for children, pets, and all other living things. Once the world ends, that's a perk, not a liability.

Leave nails, sharp tools, and open pits everywhere around your house. The pits don't even need to look like they have a purpose. People expect any home improvement project to destroy your front yard for no discernible reason. For added danger, cover the pits with soggy plywood that will collapse the first time anyone puts weight on it. Insincere attempts at safety that make your property more hazardous are a contractor specialty.

To maximize the damage potential, lay ladders on the ground next to the pits. It's impossible to step over those rungs without catching your foot and tripping. Go ahead and try. It can't be done. Unless you tried it and succeeded, in which case that trap will only stop me. Congratulations, you're safe from the author of this book. That's some peace of mind, at least.

To round out your exterior defenses, make sure your entire yard is a sea of mud. If you had the good fortune to hire a real contractor right before the zombie apocalypse, this will happen automatically. The mere presence of someone from the construction industry will cause all grass to wither and die. Scientists still don't understand why. Once this happens, your yard will remain a giant mud pool for the rest of time because good luck finding reasonably priced sod in the apocalypse. The muck will trap zombies and reduce the total area you have to mow. I wish I turned my yard into a perpetual construction site years ago. I'm sure my neighbors feel differently.

When Your Home Improvement Project Will Be Done

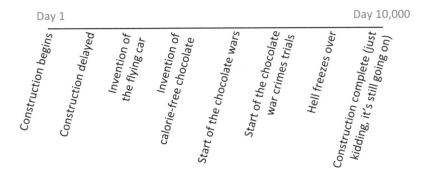

SLEEP TIGHT

The looters and monsters outside your house aren't your only problem. You also need to fear your own family. That's always true, especially during the terrible twos, but it will take on a whole new meaning during the zombie apocalypse. Since everyone who dies turns into a zombie, regardless of whether they were bitten, your spouse and kids are all potential undead adversaries. They could die at any moment from anything ranging from whooping cough to boredom. It won't be easy living with no cell service. Besides, I just told you to make the first floor of your house as dangerous as possible. The odds of it backfiring are incredibly high. In solving the problem of intruders, I created several other, much more serious problems that make the original issue seem harmless by comparison. My work here is done.

If a family member dies and comes back as a zombie during the day, it won't be a big deal. No one in your house will go quietly. Kids moan like their lives are over if they have to share their favorite crayon, so there's no way they'll secretly turn into zombies without major high-decibel water works. You'll notice. Trust me. If you find out a family member has died, calmly lock them in a closet or turn them loose to eat the neighbors. I don't recommend killing any relatives, even if they are zombies. It sets a bad example for your kids. No parent looks fully human first thing in the morning, and you don't want any misunderstandings.

If someone dies and comes back as a zombie overnight, however, it could be a disaster. As a parent, you've conditioned yourself to sleep through an inordinate amount of noise. Okay, so if you're a first-time mom or dad, you might still be in the "every noise means my child is dying" phase. But after you pump out a few more kids, you'll realize children are more durable than you thought. They might cry and scream overnight, but as long as you're confident they're still in bed, you can sleep comfortably while ignoring them. It's a good system, unless you need to listen for the pitter-patter of zombie feet.

Thankfully, there's a solution that will let you continue to tune out your children while you sleep: a loft bed. This is different from a bunk bed, which has a bed on the top and a bed on the bottom. A loft bed has a mattress on top and nothing below. In the apocalypse, loft beds won't just be for small children and poor college students anymore. No one should sleep on the ground unless they're expendable. By putting yourself up high, you'll make it harder for a zombie to bite you in the middle of the night. How effective this is depends on how far you are off the ground and the zombie's height. Tall children stop being fun to brag about when they try to eat you in your sleep.

To supplement the vertical protection of the loft, add a barrier along the edges with a gate on one end. In a normal bed, this is a handy way to keep children from falling out. In the zombie-proof variant, it turns each loft bed into a cage. Make sure the barrier runs from the loft to the ceiling to give you total protection. Just don't build these beds until after the world ends. Otherwise you'll end up on the news with all those people who make their kids sleep in dog kennels. "But it's to protect them from zombies" won't win you much sympathy in the twenty-four-hour news cycle.

If the barrier is strong enough, it will keep zombies out—or, if necessary, in. If the person in the bed dies overnight from natural causes, they'll be trapped there when they come back as an undead monster. It's a great plan, although a better one would have been to not let anyone die in the first place. Hindsight is twenty-twenty.

STAIRWAY TO HELL

As we've seen, the best homes for defense have two stories with the bottom floor in a perpetual state of disarray. Other zombie survival guides tell you to destroy the staircase to the second floor and to use a retractable ladder instead. As usual, that advice is useless for parents. Good luck climbing down narrow rungs in the dark carrying a baby. If humans were truly adapted for child rearing, we'd all have an extra set of arms.

Instead of tearing out a staircase, defend it with a series of baby gates. They're hard to get over. A looter will either stop to dismantle each one or trip over them, buying you extra time to make a stand or run away. In the case of zombies, they'll knock each gate flat and step on it. The gate will slide down the stairs like a surfboard and the zombie will topple down after it. I know this will work because I've watched it happen to more than one of my kids. Unless you're with Child Protective Services, in which case I made up that story. My children are immune to gravity.

Ladders aren't completely useless. Acquire rope ones for the second-story windows to use in case of a fire. That way you'll have another escape option besides jumping straight down and breaking every bone in your feet. Bright flames plus wounded survivors equal a zombie feeding frenzy.

Of course, even if rope ladders are readily available, kids won't use them. Following simple instructions has never been their strong suit, especially when their lives are on the line. In the highly likely event your kids either fall or jump out the window, it's a good idea to have a plan B. There are plenty of things you can put on the ground to stop your kids from dying, despite their best efforts to the contrary.

Ideal Landing Spots Beneath a Second-Story Window

Landing Surface	Pro	Con
Trampoline	You'll get an amazing second bounce.	Anyone who sets foot on one breaks at least three bones.
Mud	It's already around your house.	If you sink too deep, you'll be stationary zombie bait.
Water	Could double as a pool.	Mosquito breeding ground. Enjoy your malaria.
Ball Pit	Landing in it will be the greatest moment of your life.	You'll forget what you're running from and stay there till a zombie catches you.
Foam blocks	Used at recreational jump facilities.	Your baby will try to eat them.
Pit of Gelatin	You can eat it, though your baby won't. (They don't eat anything they're supposed to.)	The buoyancy is different than water. You'll have the most delicious drowning ever.

| Mattress | There will be a lot of them available after everybody dies. | Bedbugs are worse than zombies. |
| Haystack | Works in medieval literature. | Might land on a needle. |

READY FOR ANYTHING

All the preparations in this chapter carry a serious social stigma that will stop you from completing them ahead of time in the pre-zombie world. That's okay. As a parent with a million things to do, you're a pro at procrastinating. Flag this part of the book to find it more easily once everyone starts dying. And if your spouse suggests you do chores when the apocalypse could start at any moment, kindly point to this chapter. Cleaning your house is a sure way to kill your family.

CHAPTER 10

YOU ARE THE LAW

In a perfect world, you wouldn't need to punish your kids. Then again, in a perfect world, zombies wouldn't be walking around eating everyone. Although if you're a zombie, that's pretty much utopia.

Children will misbehave more, not less, as civilization collapses. They'll be like bulls in a china shop, but only if the bulls are actually velociraptors and those velociraptors are on meth. It's up to you to keep them in line before they destroy everything around them. The fate of the world depends on it.

It's easy to predict when your kids will act up. It will always be at the worst possible moment. Children don't put any conscious thought into picking a time. Somehow they just know. It's like how geese know to fly south every winter. Kids have a behavioral gyroscope in their brains that guides them toward being jerks at exactly the right time for them—and the wrong time for everyone else. Your children don't necessarily want to die, and they're not deliberately trying to get you killed in the process. They're just biologically programmed to act in the heat of the moment without considering the consequences. Ironically, that's how most of them were conceived in the first place.

When Kids Will Misbehave

If left unchecked, this behavior will wipe out the human race. Children who are stubborn at an inopportune moment can turn narrow escapes into gory tragedies. They never pass up a chance to make a mess. All that stands between humanity and oblivion are beleaguered parents armed with a limited arsenal of carrots and sticks. I'm speaking metaphorically, of course. In practice, real carrots and sticks are both equally ineffective. Poking a child with a branch only provokes a fit of rage, and no kid has ever stopped a temper tantrum for a vegetable.

The trick is to curb your children's behavior without accidentally killing them in the process. It's not as easy as it sounds. There's no good way to put kids in timeout while being chased by zombies. If you make your children stand in a corner to think about what they've done, you'll have to slay zombies around them the whole time. That's a lot to put yourself through just because your kid ate your last candy bar. Punishments must be dealt out sparingly and proportionately to prevent them from backfiring. Your children won't learn any valuable life lessons if they die. In fact, they'll come back as zombies, and their behavior will be more incorrigible than ever. The undead never know when to quit.

CRIME AND PUNISHMENT

The rules will be different when the world ends. Without functioning governments, there will be no one left to uphold anything. The only regulations will be the ones you put in place and enforce in your own family. Your word will be the law. Enjoy the power trip. You've earned it.

Some good, law-abiding behaviors from more civilized times will get you killed around zombies, while some former felonies will now be necessary for survival. Adjust your expectations for your kids accordingly. Save your overreactions for the right time and make them count. It's a shame to waste a good tirade.

Below are some suggestions for classic misbehaviors that should be shrugged off once the world ends. The list applies to adults as well as kids and is by no means comprehensive. Look over it and tweak it as necessary. Make the apocalypse your own.

Formerly Bad Behaviors That Are Okay in the Zombie Apocalypse

1. *Name calling*: Sticks and stones may break your bones, but words won't turn you into a shambling corpse for the rest of eternity.

2. *Swearing*: If the end of the world isn't the right time to swear, then there is no such time.

3. *Gluttony*: Your kids should eat everything they can get their hands on before it goes bad. If they eat sixteen boxes of Girl Scout cookies, they aren't pigs; they're fighters with an insatiable will to live.

4. *Lying*: Telling the truth to other groups of survivors is a sure way to get your home looted and your family murdered. Train your kids to lie like it's their job. It's an honest day's work.

5. *Stealing from strangers*: Tell your kids to always help other people. Unless those people aren't in your family. Then your kids should take everything those people have and never look back.

6. *Arson*: Burning down other houses has a strategic value. It limits zombie hiding spots and clears the field of view to watch for approaching threats. Also, it's fun and dangerous, which is every kid's dream.

7. *Murder*: When everything is out to kill your family, it's hard to get upset if your kids kill back.

Not all transgressions by your children or even other adults should be overlooked. There are some offenses that were minor in the days of law and order that will be major crimes in the time of zombies. Tell your kids about these changes up front so they can't claim they were unaware. The last thing you want is for them to get off on a technicality. And remember, all these rules also apply to you. The only thing worse than a zombie is a hypocrite.

Formerly Minor Misdeeds That Will Be Major Offenses in the Zombie Apocalypse

1. *Dawdling*: Going slowly when every second counts could get everyone killed. Plus it's annoying. Expect your kids to do it every chance they get.

2. *Not finishing their food*: You've worked too hard to keep them alive. Don't let them voluntarily starve to death. It's rude.

3. *Being loud*: Noise attracts zombies. Your kids don't have to be silent, but maybe they can hold off on the falcon mating calls for a while.

4. *Adultery*: This one was always a big deal; it just wasn't illegal before. But if you think divorces are messy in the normal world, wait until your spouse is armed at all times to fight zombies. Set a good example for your kids by not giving your other half an excuse to murder you.

5. *Cannibalism*: Full disclosure, this has always been bad. But if you were in a plane crash and stranded on a frozen mountaintop, no one would fault you if you ate a few people to survive. In the zombie apocalypse, however, that's a big no-no. It's an act of treason against the human race to imitate your zombie enemies and eat your fellow humans. If you're going to eat people, you might as well turn undead so you'll have some dinner companions.

6. *Throwing a temper tantrum*: This is the worst possible crime of the zombie apocalypse. And in a world where it won't be unheard of to kill someone over toilet paper, that's really saying something. A full-blown temper tantrum with the requisite flop on the floor and blood-curdling screams will slow a family's forward progress to a crawl. They'll either have to drag the kid kicking and screaming or stay put until the fit ends, which could last anywhere from a few minutes to the rest of the child's life. If zombies show up, those two time increments will be one and the same.

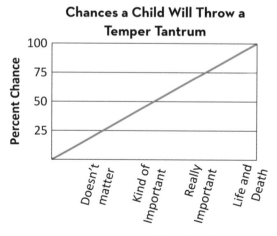

Chances a Child Will Throw a Temper Tantrum

Punishing bad behaviors and rewarding good ones will take careful balancing. Being too lenient could get your whole family killed, but so could being too strict. Death lurks behind every wrong decision. At least for once in your life there won't be any ambiguity. It will be very clear when you mess up. Look for the blood splatter.

TIME OF YOUR LIFE

Children can act like monsters even when they're still human. The go-to method to keep an out-of-control child in check has long been the timeout. Everyone does it, but no one agrees on why. Some say it's to give children time to calm down, while others insist it's to let parents cool off before they abandon their kids in the forest without any breadcrumbs. Both are plausible in the pre-zombie era. But in the apocalypse, the main goal of a timeout will be to get your children to shut up for a few minutes before they attract every zombie in the zip code. That range isn't an exaggeration. The shrill cry of children is the only sound that can penetrate the vacuum of space.

As their name suggests, the downside of timeouts is they require time. Every second you spend outside your home is potentially deadly. It's not a great time to stop and teach a life lesson. If you can't do a timeout at the moment your children cross the line, do it later. This happens all the time in the pre-zombie world. Parents let misbehavior slide in church or in a crowded store only to come down on their kids later with the wrath of an angry god—assuming an angry god lashes out by making wrongdoers stand in a corner and reflect on what they've done. For parents, the goal of this delay is to avoid causing a scene in public. In normal times, those disturbances draw every curious eyeball in the area. In the apocalypse, they'll draw every hungry mouth, too.

Your kids won't remember what's at stake. In fact, they won't remember anything. By the time you get home from running errands out on the undead hellscape, your children will have long since forgotten whatever they did wrong. Kids have selective memories, a pathological condition that often lasts a lifetime. If you tell your children to sit in a corner and think about what they've done, they'll simply dwell on the injustice of being punished for a crime they don't even remember committing. They'll view themselves as self-righteous martyrs and you as an evil and oppressive tyrant. Good work. It's better to be feared than loved.

If a timeout absolutely can't wait when you're on a supply run, be prepared for the worst. Discipline is perilous outside your home. It's hard enough to keep kids quiet and stationary in an environment with no distractions, let alone one filled with walking corpses trying to eat them. Your kids will only stay in one place if they're more afraid of you than they are of

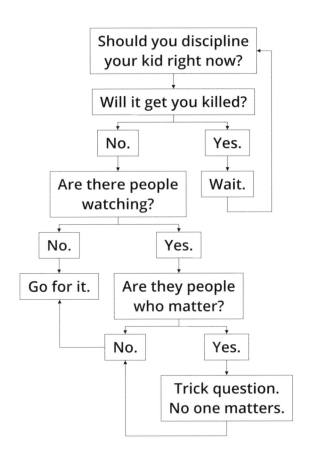

the zombies. Depending on your parenting style, that could be hard to pull off. On the grand scale of terrifying things, having your flesh ripped from your bones ranks a tad higher than being asked to stand still for some quiet soul-searching.

If you insist on doing a timeout out with zombies around, remember these dos and don'ts:

✓ **Do** explain to your children what they did wrong. If you're going to imperil their lives with a timeout, they at least deserve to know why.

✗ **Don't** tolerate any whining about the punishment. Complaining is almost as loud as a temper tantrum and will attract zombies just as fast.

✓ **Do** act like you know what you're doing. Even if you immediately realize it was dumb to do a timeout deep in zombie country, pretend it was part of your plan all along. As a parent, this is a skill you've already mastered.

✗ **Don't** be afraid to bail on the timeout if the zombie horde gets too big to fight off. Take your children with you when you run. It's bad form to let them get eaten on purpose.

✓ **Do** resume the interrupted timeout as soon as you get home. If you commute the sentence, your children will think they can get away with anything if they almost die. In the zombie apocalypse, that excuse will get old fast.

✗ **Don't** forget to use a watch. Time can seem to slow down or speed up depending on whether you're watching a pot boil or killing hordes of zombies with your family members' lives on the line. Use a timer to eliminate subjectivity. Your kids have to understand five minutes means five minutes, no matter what.

✓ **Do** threaten to do a timeout in dangerous areas again. Even if you realized it was suicidal the first time, the threat alone may be enough to deter future bad behavior. Pray your kids don't call your bluff.

- ✖ **Don't** tell your spouse what happened. There's no reason to turn a near escape into a relationship-ending fight. What your partner doesn't know could save your marriage.

HIT IT

Time to smack around a controversial topic: spanking. In a book about violently smashing zombie skulls in the presence of children, this section will still generate the most irate emails—at least until the internet goes out. I'm looking forward to the end of the world more than most.

There was a time everyone spanked their kids. Now, experts recommend against it. I'm guessing on that. I've never read a parenting book in my life, which is obvious if you've skimmed even a few pages of this guide. But in general, experts rarely recommend that you hit anything. Good luck getting by a doctoral board with the thesis "Violence is the answer."

Regardless of your feelings on spanking before the apocalypse, at the end of the world, corporal punishment should only be used as a last resort. Noise attracts zombies, and even a symbolic spanking with little force behind it will make your child cry ten times louder. This method should only be used to get your kids moving in moments of immediate peril. If a child throwing a tantrum is small enough, pick them up and carry them with you. Only use spankings if they grab onto something to hold themselves in place. That sounds farfetched to childless people, but it's a daily occurrence for parents. I've had kids grab their bed railings with their hands AND feet when I tried to get them up in the morning. I'm lucky humans no longer have prehensile tails.

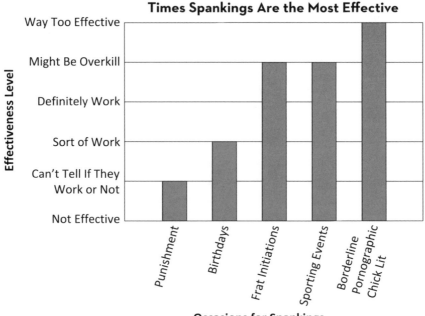

Times Spankings Are the Most Effective

Effectiveness Level (y-axis): Way Too Effective, Might Be Overkill, Definitely Work, Sort of Work, Can't Tell If They Work or Not, Not Effective

Occasions for Spankings (x-axis): Punishment, Birthdays, Frat Initiations, Sporting Events, Borderline Pornographic Chick Lit

PRIVILEGES REVOKED

There are worse things than pain. If you don't believe me, take away a teenager's phone. Or my phone for that matter. A five-minute stint in a corner might not frighten children, but a day without apps certainly will. It's a death sentence. Threaten to take away your children's electronic devices and you'll soon find you have a house full of well-behaved kids, at least until you look away.

The only problem with this approach is there won't be much left for you to revoke after the world ends. The zombies will destroy everything that makes life worth living. Even if you somehow manage to charge them, phones and tablets will be useless without the internet. I recommend holding a backyard burial for all your gadgets. It'll give your kids a sense of closure and let the grieving process begin.

To keep your punishments relevant, get creative. For teenagers, take away naps. There's nothing worse than making them stay conscious in a world they already hate. They'll have to be around their family members, who are usually their least favorite people in the world. They may also be the only people left in the world, which makes it even worse. This penalty is so devious it should be banned as cruel and unusual punishment. Too bad the Constitution will be as meaningless as those "Employees Must Wash Hands" signs. Hurray for anarchy.

The best part about nap deprivation is it's easy to enforce. Any time your teenagers fall asleep, interrupt them. Your children have been doing this to you for your entire life. It's payback time. Just don't use this punishment on younger kids. If your children are under the age of thirteen, let them rest as much as they want. That'll be the only "me time" you get in the apocalypse. Just don't spend it digging through your secret stash of junk food. Kids in a dead sleep can still hear you open a bag of chips up to four miles away.

Another effective punishment is to ban your kids from seeing their friends. This is a safe move because it means your kids will be inside your own house rather than wandering the neighborhood, risking death to improve their social lives. In all likelihood, their friends will already be undead monsters anyway. Not that this really matters. As zombies, they'll be ravenously hungry, won't think for themselves, and will have no regard for others. In other words, they'll be indistinguishable from ordinary teenagers.

The main problem with using this punishment on your kids is if their behavior improves, you'll have to let them see their friends. Going out and looking for people who may or may not still be alive is a suicide mission. Whether or not you let your kids do it will come down to how sick of them you are.

Taking away something kids already have works better than promising them something extra in the future. If you offer rewards, you'll have to constantly think of bigger and better things to keep your kids motivated. Eventually, you'll be handing out expensive watches and luxury sedans when your kids do the dishes. Most of that stuff will be free through looting, but getting it will be a lot of work and storage space might become an issue. If you just take away something your kids already have, you can give it back when they stop acting up. Plus you can do that an infinite number of times without taking up any more garage bays.

EXTRA CHORES

If you want to kill two birds with one stone, punish your kids with chores. Of course, literally killing two birds with one stone would be even better because then your family could eat. If your kids do ever get a double bird kill with a single rock, give them a full pardon for whatever they did. Food trumps everything. Plus that would mean they've got one heck of an arm. You don't want them to hate you if the apocalypse ends and they become rich professional athletes.

There will be more than enough work to go around after the end of the world, so using chores for a punishment seems like a no-brainer. Once the running water stops, you'll have to go somewhere with buckets to fetch it. There will be laundry to wash by hand, supplies to gather, food to cook, and a house to clean—if only the second floor, as I explained in the home defense chapter. You'll be amazed how dirty a place gets when an entire family is home all day to mess it up. Keeping even part of it clean might not be possible. At some point, it may be better to burn it down and move.

Feel free to dump as many of these chores on your kids as you can. The worse your kids are, the less you'll have to do. There will finally be an upside to having terrible children.

Top Chores to Use as Punishment

Chore	Pro	Con
Carrying Water	Your kids will stay hydrated.	The water will come back soaked in their clothes, not in the buckets.
Cooking Dinner	For once, you can complain about someone else's cooking.	It's dangerous to put a person who's mad at you in charge of your food.
Doing Laundry	You can make someone else drag all your laundry to the river and stand in it for hours.	Your kids might get swept away or, worse, have fun in the water.
Doing the Dishes	Kids are a convenient replacement for the dishwasher.	You might not have enough food to get the dishes dirty.
Going on Supply Runs	Your kids will find new stuff to bring home.	They'll lose it all on the way back. The apocalypse won't have a lost and found.
Inventory the Supplies	It'll keep the pantry organized.	It'll keep your pantry mysteriously empty.
Cleaning the House	It's their mess anyway.	They'll make the house dirty at roughly the same rate they clean, so the best you can hope for is that they break even.

Gathering Firewood	It'll help heat your home.	It'll help your kids burn stuff.
Cleaning the Windows	The glass will sparkle like never before.	No one will notice since you'll have blankets over it.

Like timeouts, chores are a delayed punishment. If your kids act up when you're out in the open surrounded by zombies, you can't make them wash windows right then. You'll have to wait until you get home. To be effective, the prospect of doing a chore in the future has to be so unpleasant that even the threat of it forces immediate obedience. That means chores that are even a little fun can't be punishments. If your kids like to carry water buckets or cook food, don't let them do either. Your job is to squeeze all the joy out of their lives. It shouldn't be hard. You're probably doing it already.

There are some chores that should never be used as a punishment, even if kids hate them. These include patrolling the perimeter, night guard duty, and scouting the surrounding area to check for zombie swarms and hostile groups of survivors. Kids doing anything as a punishment will do a bad job. It's not a huge issue if they only clean half the laundry or retrieve half the needed amount of water, but if they only patrol half the perimeter, everyone might wake up as zombies. Never put your kids in charge of anything your life depends on. That's a good rule to live by even in the pre-zombie world.

Along the same lines, don't punish your kids with any chores that put something sharp or deadly in their hands. Kids are unfocused even when they're perfectly serene. Add in anger and disobedience, and their attention to detail will dip. Only send your children to chop wood as a punishment if you're fine with them coming home with fewer limbs than they started with. If your child has a limb surplus, that might work out, but if your kid has the standard number, leave chopping to the professionals.

The downside of using chores as a punishment is eventually you'll become reliant on your children's help. If you make chores a penalty for bad behavior and your kids stop misbehaving, you'll have to do all that work yourself. It's a system that encourages your kids to act better but incentivizes you to keep them bad. The only workaround to this problem is to punish your kids with made-up chores that don't really need to be done. Figuring out what to make your kids do will be harder than doing all the chores yourself. So you can either create more work for yourself or you can let your kids get away with everything. There are no wins in parenting.

UNDER MY ROOF

Many children threaten to run away. Very few go through with it. Deep down, they know they have a sweet deal at home. There are only two people in the world who love them by default. Yes, sometimes kids end up with only one, and in some hard circumstances they have none. But for most children, there are two parents who would literally die for them. It isn't merit-based. Kids don't have to earn love like a spouse does. If kids slack off, their parents can't divorce them. The closest equivalent is giving them up for adoption, but the age limit for that cuts off early. Not that I've looked into it or anything.

It's crazy for a kid to give up their built-in servants, but some children still threaten to do it. They think they'll get a better deal in a cold, uncaring world where no one will notice if they live or die. Most kids realize their mistake before they get to the front door, although a few make it down the street or to a neighbor's house. The only thing worse than living at home is living somewhere else.

Under your roof, you make the rules. Kids try to find loopholes—whether those rules apply on lawns and in courtyards is a constant source of debate—but in general, the principle is universally accepted. So if you have older children who refuse to follow your rules, the ultimate disciplinary measure is to make them move out. Your teenagers or almost-adult children will undoubtedly think this is a good idea at first. So you have to make sure they're self-sufficient enough to survive until they learn their lesson. If they walk out the door and get eaten by zombies right away, you'll have accomplished nothing. Although as a parent, you should be used to that by now.

Also, make sure you're prepared in the unlikely event your children thrive on their own and don't come back. At that point, you've technically succeeded as a parent. Against all odds, you somehow managed to raise self-sufficient human beings. Of course, if you kicked them out during the zombie apocalypse, they'll hate your guts forever. That's okay. It shows they're excellent judges of character.

LIFE LESSONS

No matter which punishment you choose, it'll only be effective if your kids understand why they're in trouble. After the offense and punishment have both run their course, sit your children down and explain to them why you did what you did. Your kids will listen intently and say they understand. Then they'll act up again. If punishing kids actually worked, half the parents in America wouldn't self-medicate with alcohol. But you have to stick with it. Maybe your children will learn to behave because you're a stern disciplinarian. Or maybe they'll grow up on their own. Either way, most kids get there eventually. And those that don't go into politics.

Even if none of your attempts at discipline work, at least you tried. You can struggle through the zombie apocalypse knowing that for all the things that are wrong with your kids, your parenting wasn't the problem. Their bad attitudes probably come down to genetics, and that's only fifty percent your fault.

CHAPTER 11

SO YOU HAVE TO CUT OFF YOUR ARM

Sometimes the worst happens. Scratch that. Usually the worst happens. That's the second rule of parenting. The first rule is if the kids are quiet, they're up to something.

In a world full of ravenous undead monsters, the odds of being bitten by a zombie are high. Add a distracting kid to the mix, and the chances skyrocket. It's hard to keep an eye out for reanimated corpses while also arguing with a four-year-old about whether or not her leggings are the right shade of pink. At least you'll die over something important.

But if you are bitten by a zombie, don't give up yet. You have one small chance of survival: amputation. Cut off the bitten area immediately before the infection spreads. Read this section in advance to save precious seconds. If you've already been bitten and you're perusing it for the first time right now, it's too late. Unless you're a speed reader. I should probably stop using all these extra words to slow you down. Right after this sentence. Or maybe this one. Moan if you're dead yet.

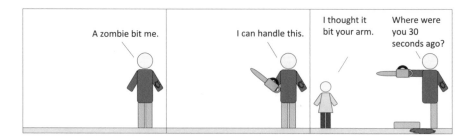

Once you're bitten, you'll have only moments to make several life-or-death decisions. That's why it's important to plan them out ahead of time. Sit down with your family and decide which limbs you can and can't live without. Write down your decision, preferably on a crude, cartoonish drawing your kids can understand. They might be the only ones around to do the cutting. Make your instructions comprehensive and legible. You won't be able to give any last-minute instructions. Your kids won't hear you over the chainsaw.

This is the amputation chart I gave to my family:

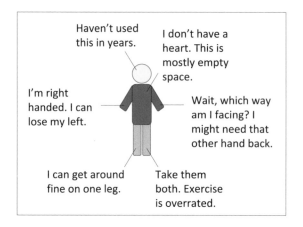

SLICE AND DICE

Always keep a sharp cutting tool nearby. It's best to have it somewhere on your person. If you set it down, you'll never see it again. You have kids in the house, so things move on their own. It's like living with poltergeists.

Having the right tool at hand the moment you need it will make all the difference. It doesn't matter if you were only bitten on your pinkie. You'll still die if the sharpest cutting tool available is a spoon. Unless you're tough enough to slowly scoop off your own hand. Remember me when you get your movie deal.

Whatever you use will be subpar by modern surgery standards. There won't be many sanitized scalpels floating around once the dead walk the earth. Then again, you also won't end up hundreds of thousands of dollars in debt. Insurance companies won't survive the zombie apocalypse. The end of the world sounds kind of nice.

The Best Cutting Tools

Cutting Tool	Pro	Con
Butter Knife	Great if you want to butter a scone for your last meal.	You won't live long enough to eat it.
Steak Knife	Sharp.	Hard to use effectively without a fork to hold your limb in place.
Karate Chop	If this works, you're the most deadly ninja ever to live.	It won't.
Wolverine's Claws	You're Wolverine in the X-Men.	Nothing can slice off your arm. Your adamantium skeleton prevents it.
Sheet of Paper	If you rub your finger on it just right, it's the sharpest cutting surface on earth.	Literally death by a thousand cuts.
Machete	Great for strong, swift blows.	Messy. Stock up on stain remover.
Chainsaw	Fast.	Will attract zombies with noise and splatter.
Industrial Cutting Laser	The closest you'll come in real life to getting your hand chopped off by a lightsaber.	Needs electricity. Good luck finding enough AA batteries.
Clamshell Packaging	Has cut off countless fingers in vain attempts to open it.	Your profuse bleeding will ruin whatever's inside.

THE MOMENT AFTER

So let's say you've been bitten. The first thing you need to do is eliminate the zombie threat. If there's only one zombie that snuck up on you, kill it as quickly as possible. It's hard to perform life-saving surgery if there's still a monster actively eating you. If there are a bunch of zombies, on the other hand, retreat to a safe location. Resist the urge to stay put and make a heroic last stand. You have kids to think of. They're the perfect excuse for cowardice.

Once you're out of immediate danger, assess the wound. If it's in one of the areas you can't live without, settle in for a painful death. You might have a day or two to kill. I hope you brought snacks and board games. Trivial Pursuit is a good choice. It'll make dying seem great by comparison.

If the bite is in a zone you deem expendable, however, it's time to pick a surgeon. This is something you can't prepare for in advance because you have no idea who will be with you at the time. Given that this is the zombie apocalypse, your odds of an actual doctor being there are negligible. Even if there is one, I don't recommend using them. They'll expect some kind of compensation in the new barter economy. Living is hardly worth it if you have to part with your last pack of diapers.

If you're like most parents, you don't have time for friends. That narrows down who might be with you if you get bitten. Realistically, there are three possibilities: (1) your spouse; (2) your kids; (3) no one. Each situation comes with its own perils.

If you choose your spouse, you'll have someone with strong, competent hands to guide the cutting tool. If you've argued with them in the last twenty-four hours, you'll also have someone with the right incentive. Just make sure they're not angry enough to want you dead. A good marriage walks the fine line between mild annoyance and homicidal intent.

How to Have Your Spouse Cut Off Your Arm

1. Verify your spouse is mad enough to wound but not to kill.
2. Ask nicely.
3. Tie a tourniquet around the part you want cut off.
4. Remind them that if you die, they'll have to raise all the kids by themselves.
5. Close your eyes.
6. Open them.
7. Count how many body parts you have left.

Letting your kids perform the amputation has its own perils. You've seen how much damage they can cause with safety scissors. Now imagine a kindergartner with a battle ax. That's why I have nightmares. If your children are a little older, however, they might be able to pull it off. Ideally, pick a kid who's too old to hate you for early bedtimes but too young to hate you for early curfews. The age of twelve is about perfect. They still care enough to try to impress you, but they don't understand how life insurance policies work yet.

How to Have Your Child Cut Off Your Arm

1. Hand them the cutting tool.
2. Explain that you cut them out of your will, but you'll put them back in it if you survive this.
3. Hope this isn't a repeat of the time you let them carve the turkey and spent the rest of the day cleaning shredded meat off the ceiling.

The final option is to cut off your own arm. Before you attempt this, you'll be filled with self-doubt. This is justified. You know all your own faults. It's a good thing you've never had to write yourself a letter of recommendation.

Cutting off your own arm is not for the faint of heart. Actually, it might be. A weak heart pumps blood slower, so it'll take you longer to bleed out. Although that's not necessarily a good thing. It means if you fail, you'll suffer in agony for longer before you die and become a zombie. Only cut off an arm or a leg if you're seriously committed to living through it. If you die anyway, you've doomed yourself to an eternity as a one-armed zombie. Good luck being taken seriously as a predator.

How to Cut Off Your Own Arm

1. Take a swig of the strongest alcohol you can find.
2. Take another swig.
3. Finish the bottle.
4. Finish several other bottles.
5. Pass out.
6. Wake up as a zombie.

Clearly that didn't go as planned. Cutting off your own arm is a lot harder than it sounds.

Adjust the amount of alcohol you consume until you hit the sweet spot where you can't feel anything but you're still awake. This will take a lot of preparation beforehand. Practice drinking weeks or months in advance. If your spouse disapproves, tell them to back off. This isn't alcoholism; it's advanced first aid.

Whatever you do, don't try to outdo that one guy who famously cut off his own arm after a boulder fell on it. He was young and fit. You're a parent. Physical pain is easy to cope with if it's not accompanied by the overwhelming emotional trauma of raising tiny people you created. Besides, zombies weren't around back then. If that guy had died, he would have stayed dead, not turned into a walking corpse. Talk about no pressure.

No matter who you choose as your amateur surgeon, before anyone starts cutting, keep these pointers in mind:

✓ **Do** conduct the amputation outside to reduce cleanup. Carpet stains are a pain to get out.

✗ **Don't** scream too loudly. Put something in your mouth to sink your teeth into. Make sure it isn't someone else's arm. That's how misunderstandings happen.

✓ **Do** keep the amputated limb for a while. When you meet someone new, act like it's still attached. Shake their hand. Pretend to freak out when they pull off your arm.

✗ **Don't** keep it forever. The smell will attract hungry mouths, both living and dead. Zombies will be the least of your problems if you're surrounded by the world's last bears.

✓ **Do** keep a positive attitude. Kids learn by example. If they see you complain, they'll whine even more than they do now. You'll wish you'd died on the operating table.

✗ **Don't** get frustrated if you can't do everything you used to do. Outside pursuits are for childless people. If an amputation didn't destroy your hobbies, your kids would've anyway.

✓ **Do** milk the situation for everything it's worth. You don't get very many legitimate excuses to get out of housework. For once, you have very clear-cut evidence you're not faking it.

✗ **Don't** expect it to work. You still have one working arm. Pick up after yourself, you worthless slob.

THE ROAD TO RECOVERY

The next steps will depend on what got cut off. If you lost an arm, walk it off. If you lost a leg, hop it off. That's the best medical care you can hope for at this point. If you're lucky, you can stop the bleeding with gauze or maybe some duct tape. Whatever you do, don't cauterize the wound. You'll set yourself on fire. The zombie apocalypse is hard enough without also having your entire body covered in third-degree burns. Then again, zombies might leave you alone. They'll smell from a distance that you're overcooked.

Keep in mind the amputation might not have been enough and you could still die from infection. Or it might have been too much and the amputation itself could kill you. Either way, you'll come back as a zombie. Be sure to have someone standing nearby to bash in your head if necessary. That's what family is for.

A HELPING CUT

Amputations are sort of like Christmas presents: It's better to give than to receive. If someone near you is bitten, be prepared to chop off their limbs. It's the neighborly thing to do. For your spouse, the process should be easy enough. Switch the roles listed in the steps above. You'll say you feel their pain, but that's a lie. Real pain hurts a hell of a lot more than empathy.

Conversely, amputating a child's limb will require substantial adjustments to the plan. Kids get sentimental about things like a beloved blanket or a favorite arm or leg. Cutting something off might prove traumatic. Sit the child down. Look them squarely in the eye. Then lie. Lie like you've never lied before. Lie like their little life depends on it, because it does. Tell them to close their eyes because you're giving them a present, you're playing hide and go seek, or there's an ugly naked person you don't want them to see. If they've ever seen you undress, they'll know the last one might not be a bluff. Whatever the excuse, the second they close their eyes, hack off the infected part. It's best to use a machete or ax so you can do it in one swift, concise motion. That way they won't be tipped off. It's hard to surprise someone with a weed whacker.

Afterward, there will be a few tears. Okay, maybe more than a few. But if you've been a parent for any length of time, you should be immune to them by now. Kids cry about nothing and everything and all the stuff in between. I've been dealing with it for so long that I almost forgot desperate sobbing isn't a normal reaction to having a sandwich cut into triangles. Apparently rectangles taste better. This time, your kid will have something worth crying about. But tell them to put a sock in it so they don't attract the undead. Then give them a sock to bite on. Just tell them not to clamp down too hard. In the barter economy, goods will be scarce, and saving a life won't be worth ruining a perfectly wearable pair of socks.

WE CAN REBUILD HIM

An amputation doesn't have to be a bad thing. Don't look at it as losing a limb; look at it as gaining a slot for accessories. Chopping off a hand is a great chance to build a tool directly into your wrist. The classic choice is a metal hook. It's great for stabbing things, but it's less than ideal if you need to hold a baby. Then again, you'll probably be off diaper duty for life.

There are plenty of other ways to trick out a new stump. The goal is to permanently graft something to your body that's equally useful for zombie murder and daily family life.

Best Attachments for an Arm Stump

Attachment	Pro	Con
Hook	Great for terrifying teenagers at Makeout Point.	Fatal if your nose itches.
Closed Metal Fist	Great for fist bumping.	Subpar for high-fives.
Nunchuck	Looks good with every outfit.	100 percent chance of hitting yourself in vital reproductive areas.
Megaphone	Great for yelling at kids.	Even better at attracting zombies.
Dagger	Great if you need to dice a salad.	Awkward if you need to shake hands.
Handgun	No one will ask you to babysit.	High likelihood of an accident when playing "pull my finger."
Flamethrower	Roasted marshmallows anytime you want.	Having fuel tanks strapped to your back is bad for your posture and love life.
Snack Cup	Snacks.	Corn chip supply not guaranteed.

Best Attachment for a Leg Stump

Attachment	Pro	Con
No Replacement, Just Crutches	You can sword-fight whenever you want.	Everyone will feel bad and talk about how brave you are.
Standard Prosthetic Leg	Toes can't be stubbed.	One of your kids will inevitably steal it and make you kick your own butt.
Peg Leg	You'll look like a pirate.	Vulnerable to beavers. Like you need another predator to worry about.
Pogo Stick	You'll finally be able to dunk.	Haven't existed outside cartoons since 1952.
Giant Exercise Ball	You'll have a strong core.	To fit it, you'll have to cut off both legs and attach it directly to your torso.
Novelty Lamp That Looks Like a Woman's Leg	It will be mildly funny the first time you use it.	It will immediately shatter, causing massive lacerations. Probably still worth it.
Machine Gun	They did it in a movie, so it must be possible.	Accidental firings are hard on wood floors.
Wheels	Great for going down hills.	You'll look like a Segway, eliminating any chance of ever getting laid again.

LESS IS MORE

Honestly, losing a limb might be the best thing that could happen to you. Use your new attachments to achieve your full potential as a parent/zombie-killing warrior. That's the coolest you'll ever be. And when your new replacement limb is detached, you might finally hit your goal weight. Amputation isn't just about surviving. It's about being fashion forward. Enjoy the new you.

CHAPTER 12

DRIVING OFF INTO THE SUNSET

There's one secret about the zombie apocalypse I've saved till the end. I wanted to make sure you were ready. For the past eleven chapters, you've learned how to slowly and arduously survive the daily grind of the zombie apocalypse. Now here's how to tackle it in easy mode.

Warning: Extreme hype ahead. If you have a heart condition, this section might kill you. Read it anyway. Some things are worth dying for. This is one of them.

So it's the zombie apocalypse and you're tired of walking. Get a minivan. You heard me right. You can hoof it forever like a poor person or you can ride to Valhalla on a unicorn. Yes, I called a minivan a unicorn. It can be whatever it wants to be. It's the chariot of the gods. Humans asked Prometheus for fire, and he said, "Screw that." Then he went back up to Mount Olympus and stole a minivan. People were so psyched they didn't even notice they still had no way to cook their food. They watched *Finding Nemo* on the built-in DVD player until they all starved to death. And it was good.

But a minivan can't be a unicorn all the time. It's too busy being a four-wheeled sex machine. Everyone who drives one has been laid AT

LEAST once. You can't own one of these bad boys unless you have kids. It's illegal. Sitting in the driver's seat is like a Bat Signal that screams to the world, "MY REPRODUCTIVE ORGANS ARE IN WORKING ORDER." I don't care if the Bat Signal doesn't make any noise. When you drive a minivan, you can hear light. Birds spent millions of years evolving colorful feathers to attract a mate; all you had to do was turn the key in the ignition. Vroom vroom.

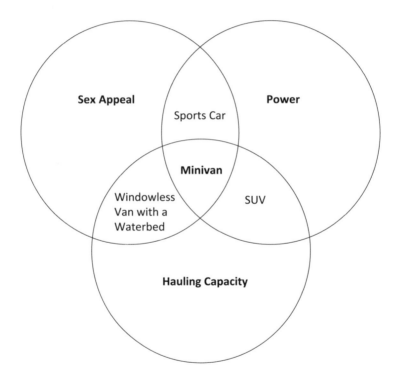

"Sex machine" isn't just a name. It will really get you laid. Like, so much so it'll be a problem. Families are like fish: They grow to the size of their container. With an eight-passenger minivan, you upgrade from a goldfish bowl to an eighty-gallon aquarium. Expect your partner to jump on you the second you pull into your driveway. It's pretty much going to be all sex all the time after that. After the first few days, you won't even remember how to stand. Don't worry about minor details like pregnancy and childbirth. With a minivan, new kids just kind of materialize in their car seats like they beamed down from the *Enterprise*. This is true even if you're in a relationship in which kids should be impossible. When you own a minivan, life finds a way. Your ride will be filled to capacity in no time. Then you can get back to surviving. Just don't get a van that holds more than eight passengers. You don't have time for that much sex. There's an apocalypse going on.

The sex isn't even the best reason to own a minivan. Hell, it doesn't make the top ten. I'd put it at around number twelve or thirteen, depending on how I feel at any given moment about stow-and-go seating. Driving a minivan is better than sex. When married couples have really good sex, they say, "That was ALMOST as good as a minivan." The only thing better than driving a minivan is driving it some more. Or maybe driving two minivans at once. I don't think that's even possible, but it should be. Get on it, scientists.

If you're a non-minivan driver, right now you're shaking your head in confusion. "But I test-drove a minivan once," you say to yourself. "It wasn't that great." Wrong. YOU weren't that great. The wand chooses the wizard, Harry. If you drove a minivan and you didn't enjoy it, you were not worthy. You didn't reject the minivan. The minivan rejected you. Have fun being a muggle.

To enjoy a minivan, you have to be dead inside. Not sort of sad or discouraged, but all the way dead. Like the doctor slaps the defibrillator on your soul and shouts "CLEAR!" but instead of coming back to life your soul catches fire like dried balsa wood. Then some jaded nurse flushes the ashes down a toilet. THAT is how dead you have to be inside to be worthy of a minivan.

Dying on the inside isn't a bad thing. It's a rite of passage. You don't become a Navy SEAL by showing up to an ice cream social and writing your name on the signup sheet. You become one by going through months and months of hellish training that weeds out all but the toughest sons of guns on the planet. Parenting works the same way. Those who can't cut it buy crossover hatchbacks that match their antidepressant bottles. But those who can stare into the existential abyss that is child rearing without blinking, well, they're worthy of a higher ride.

"Okay," you say to yourself, "a minivan is a great ride. But what's that have to do with the zombie apocalypse?" It's like you haven't heard a word I've said. Probably because these words are printed on a page and don't make sound. Go back and read this chapter out loud. Actually, shout it. The only reason I didn't type this entire thing in all caps is I slammed my keyboard so hard I broke the caps-lock key.

If you want to go anywhere in the zombie apocalypse, you need a minivan. Do you know how much stuff you can cram into one? A lot. Like, a boatload, which is like a regular load, but proportioned for a boat. That's right, I went nautical. You can shove in all the blankets and pacifiers and stuffed animals your kids need plus knives and booze, too. Think you can put all that stuff in a sedan? No way. If you jam all that stuff in a four-door car, there won't be room for oxygen. Do you want to hold your breath for the entire zombie apocalypse? I didn't think so.

A minivan has room for luggage. It has room for air. And it has room for liquids. That's right: It has space for THREE states of matter. Kids shoot liquid out of every orifice, and it constantly needs to be replenished. The minivan knows that. It knows everything. Each minivan has at least twelve state-of-the-art liquid stabilization chambers, known to commoners as cup holders. That's way more than any other vehicle. It's basically a cup holder collection with an engine attached. If you want to, you can haul a dozen slushies at once. Can't find a slushie after the end of the world? Not my problem. I don't have problems. I drive a minivan.

Don't want to spend the end of the world drinking happiness in liquid form? How about watching a film instead? Minivans are mobile movie theaters. Once the world ends, they'll have the last working TVs on the planet. There won't be electricity anywhere else. Sure, you could try a portable DVD player, but AA batteries run out fast, and new ones corrode in the package. Besides, portable DVD players barely exist anymore already. You might as well scrounge up an eight-track player and a sundial while you're at it. "But what about my phone?" you say. "Can't I charge it in the van and use that?" What you are you going to watch on it, smart guy? Phones don't have a DVD slot. Minivans do. It's like they were built for the apocalypse.

But I can still hear doubters. "You're just ranting about sex machines," they say. "We want facts." Well, strap in because I'm about to take you on a wild ride to Truth Town, population: you. That's right, you're moving in. I already informed the post office. Two quick points for the naysayers: (1) You're wrong. (2) You're wrong. That was actually the same point twice, but the second time was slightly more condescending. Minivan drivers got that. We understand each other. We understand everything.

The anti-minivan crowd always starts with same argument. "I don't need a minivan to haul my family," they say. "I'm too cool for that. I'll drive an SUV." So what happens if you follow through? Congratulations, you bought a lie. If you think that makes you young and hip, you're driving 4,000 pounds of pure self-delusion. It's a heavier, slower minivan with worse gas mileage and double the price tag. The only reason to own one is to show off to other people. Spoiler alert: No one cares. They'll be too focused on being eaten by the undead. Soon you'll join them thanks to your poor vehicle choice. And when that happens, minivan owners won't stop to help. They'll be too distracted by what's happening to Nemo.

"But, but, but," you stammer, oh unfortunate SUV owner, "SUVs can tow stuff." What are you going to tow in the zombie apocalypse? Here's a great idea: Let's attach a giant trailer to the back of a large, slow SUV to make it even larger and slower. That totally won't get you attacked by other survivors or the undead. Also, why do you have so much stuff that you need a trailer? Declutter a little. It's the end of the world. You don't need to take the china hutch.

"But," you say even more defiantly, "SUVs can go off-road." Really? When's the last time you saw an SUV drive anywhere that wasn't a road? America has millions of miles of streets and highways, and once everyone dies, they'll be largely abandoned. But instead of driving on these gigantic concrete thoroughfares that span the entire country, you want to go driving through some bean field? Okay, have fun. Guess what? In 100 yards, you'll run into another road. Might as well drive on it—but only if you make it there. SUVs have power, but they also have weight. There's a good chance you'll sink in the mud and get stuck. Then who you gonna call? Read the fine print on your AAA card. It's null and void at the end of the world.

"But," you say yet again in a huffier voice, "SUVs are better for ramming zombies." Let's break this down. When's the last time you saw an SUV driver ram a deer on purpose just because they could? Never? That's because living matter wrecks SUVs just like it wrecks everything else. Zombies are bigger than deer. Have you looked around lately? We're not a country of small people. Finding someone who weighs less than 300 pounds is like spotting Sasquatch. How are you going to run that over? It's like hitting a wall made of ham.

"But," you say for at least the millionth time in a row, "if SUVs aren't the answer, surely there must be something else I can drive." Let's consult the chart. It's not just any chart. It's a chart printed in a book. That means every word of it is true.

Best Vehicles in the Zombie Apocalypse

Vehicle	Pro	Con
Horse	Doesn't take gas.	Will serve as an appetizer for zombies before they eat you.
Bicycle	Fast on paved surfaces.	Hard seat will make you envy the dead.
Dirt Bike	Great for pointlessly jumping small hills.	Loud enough to attract every zombie in a three-mile radius.
Motorcycle	Looks cool.	You'll die if you hit anything larger than a squirrel.

Sedan	Easy to get one since they're everywhere.	Can only fit all your stuff inside if you leave your children behind.
SUV	Great if you need to tow a boat.	Zombie apocalypse will limit chances for aquatic recreation.
Tank	Invincible death machine.	There won't be enough gas left in the world to drive it off the parking lot.
Minivan	Will keep your children alive.	So perfect it hurts.

There it is in black and white. A minivan is better than every single vehicle out there. And why wouldn't it be? It's not a single vehicle. It's a transformer. Fold down the seats or take them out and BOOM, you've got a truck. I used mine to haul lumber for a 240-foot-long fence. Sure, the men at the hardware store laughed at me behind my back—and to my face and to both sides of me—but their ignorance isn't my problem. Once the zombies come, those jerks will wish they had my minivan's transitional hauling capacity. I may or may not have yelled that as I drove away. And that's why I can never go back.

The minivan is also a combat aircraft. Other than the missiles. And the flying. But its dual sliding doors open like an attack helicopter's. Swoop into a hostile environment with the doors wide open. Your armed party can jump into battle while the minivan is still rolling. Those sliding doors are stealthy, too. They open with a whisper at the touch of a button. A minivan is a ninja. I'd show you to prove it, but you couldn't see it. That's the point.

"But how will you power this ninja attack helicopter?" the doubters ask. Easy. It runs on pure adrenaline. And regular unleaded fuel. But mostly adrenaline. Unlike an SUV, a minivan gets great gas mileage, so there'll be more than enough processed petroleum to keep it going. You just have to know where to look. Start with other people's garages. A vehicle left inside was likely parked there on purpose and still has gas, as opposed to one abandoned on the road, which someone probably drove until the gas ran out. More importantly, many garages have beer fridges. The power won't be on, but a warm bottle is better than none at all. Drink until you believe that lie.

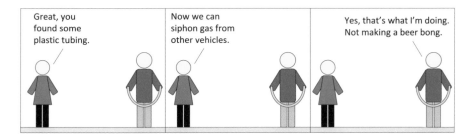

So what have you learned today? The world is full of big, powerful vehicles that seem perfect for the post-apocalyptic wasteland. Every single one of them will get you killed. Only the minivan has what it takes to keep your family safe from zombie hordes. It offers the right combination of protection, power, and hauling capacity to get your loved ones to hell and back—and then back to hell one more time because your kid forgot a stuffed animal there. Heaven forbid she ride out the apocalypse without Mr. Fluffers.

Sedans, trucks, SUVs, and all two-wheeled vehicles are nothing but high-end death traps. If your goal is to look stylish while zombies rend you and your family to pieces, by all means splurge for that brand-new truck you saw advertised between two erectile-dysfunction commercials. But if you want your family to make it to tomorrow, put them in a minivan. You'll all survive, even if you're dead inside.

THE END OF THE END

If you made it to this chapter, pat yourself on the back. Actually, pat me on the back. I kept you alive for the length of this book. Let's be honest: You're as surprised as I am. Neither of us expected this guide to be useful. Maybe you got it as a gift from someone who hates you. Or perhaps you picked it up to see if anyone hollowed it out and hid a flask. But whatever the reason, twelve chapters later, you're still with me, upright and breathing. Those extra minutes are nothing to scoff at. Too bad you spent them all reading this book.

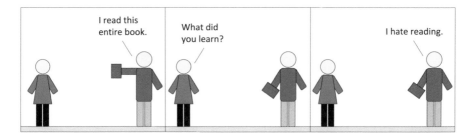

It's possible I don't deserve all the credit for your survival—although I'm claiming it anyway. Maybe you're still alive simply because nothing has had a chance to kill you. If the zombie apocalypse hasn't reached your area yet, don't get cocky. Soon you'll have to put my strategies into practice. If you think my ideas sound bad now, wait until the survival of your family depends on them. I hope you read that panic section closely.

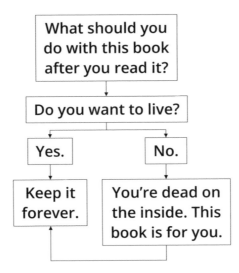

So let's say the zombie apocalypse already happened. What's next? That depends on your outlook on life. If you're an optimist, you just have to keep your family alive until the world is up and running again. For the first time in history, people won't exploit a worldwide tragedy for their personal gain. Instead, they'll put aside their petty differences, slay all the zombies, and rebuild civilization with a new sense of camaraderie and purpose. Of course, it won't all be easy. Your hand will hurt from too many high-fives, and you'll lose your voice after the one millionth round of "Kumbaya." To reach this future, all you'll need to do is believe in humanity. And fairies, pixies, and unicorns.

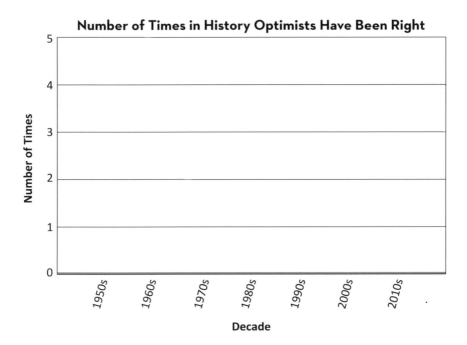

Number of Times in History Optimists Have Been Right

y-axis: Number of Times (0–5)

x-axis: Decade — 1950s, 1960s, 1970s, 1980s, 1990s, 2000s, 2010s

If you're a pessimist, you know the only time things stop being bad is when they get worse. Once civilization collapses, it'll be gone for good. It was only held together by dental floss and glue in the first place. There's no way to put it back together again. It's outside the warranty period, and replacing it with a newer model isn't in the budget. Once the world collapses, the hellish dystopia that takes its place will be here for good. That much should be obvious from the start. That's why it's called the zombie apocalypse, not the zombie temporary setback.

But even in the worst-case scenario, there's an upside. If the world never bounces back, it'll take the pressure off you as a parent. You won't have to worry about your children competing with other kids socially or academically. Peer pressure will end with the deaths of their peers, and scholastic rivalries will be buried with them. There won't be any more prestigious universities with a limited number of available slots. Instead, education will be more personal and practical. Teach your kids to do the basics—reading and writing for lists of punishment chores, counting for diaper trades, etc.—and they'll be fine. Your parenting will be judged solely on a pass/fail basis. If your kids are still alive, you did a good job. And if they're not alive, you still probably did a good job. There's a 99 percent chance if they died, it's their own fault. Remember that when you meet them again as zombies.

So what were you supposed to take away from this book? Probably nothing. If people were capable of learning from their mistakes, the world would be full of only children. So why did I write this guide at all? To be honest, I didn't set out to help people. When I started this book, my motives were strictly financial. But now that I've finished it, well, my motives are exactly the same. Sorry if you expected me to have an epiphany. Writing a book didn't make me a better person, just a slightly less poor one. If you want character growth, stick to the fiction section. Still, it makes me feel good to know you and your family survived because of me. Of course, if at some point you stop surviving, I'll feel good, too. Then I can loot your stuff. In hindsight, giving away all these tips was a bad idea. All I did was help my competition.

ACKNOWLEDGMENTS

Writing a book is a group effort. The following people deserve a share of the credit. And the blame.

- My literary agent, Mark Gottlieb of Trident Media Group. This isn't the most commercially viable book concept I could have chosen, but it's the one I wanted to write. Thanks for supporting my bad decision making. You're the perfect enabler.
- Glenn Yeffeth, publisher of BenBella Books. I don't know why you took a chance on this book when so many other publishers passed. Maybe you saw something in me that everyone else missed. Or maybe you lost a bet. Either way, this book wouldn't exist without you gambling on a first-time author with a weird idea. Hopefully I don't ruin us both.
- Leah Wilson, BenBella editor in chief. I admire your grace and professionalism in the face of insurmountable absurdity. I made up all this stuff off the top of my head. Then you had to critique the logic of it line by line for 200 pages. It occurs to me now that this book, while the high point of my life, was probably the low point of yours. Thanks for toughing it out. I don't owe you a drink; I owe you the entire bottle.
- My wife and kids. I complained about your interference constantly, but the truth is this book wouldn't exist without you. I base all

my jokes on your daily antics. Without that material, I'd have no audience, and without that audience, I'd have no book. Thanks for putting up with me for the months and months it took me to write this. I promise to never put you through that again. At least not until the sequel.

ABOUT THE AUTHOR

James Breakwell is a professional comedy writer and amateur father of four girls, ages seven and under. He is best known for his family humor Twitter account @XplodingUnicorn, which has more than 885,000 followers. The account went viral in April 2016 thanks to a feature article on the front page of BuzzFeed. The resulting attention from media outlets around the world transformed Mr. Breakwell from a niche comedy writer into one of the most famous dads on social media.

Mr. Breakwell has been profiled by *USA TODAY*, *Us Weekly*, *Daily Mail*, *Metro*, the *Telegraph*, *Cosmopolitan*, *Better Homes and Gardens*, The

Huffington Post, Upworthy, theCHIVE, Bored Panda, various ABC and FOX TV news affiliates, and countless other TV, radio, and internet outlets. Pictures of his smiling girls have been displayed in newspapers as far away as India. His articles have appeared in *Reader's Digest*, the *Federalist*, and AskMen. He has been a guest multiple times on HLN's *The Daily Share*, and the show hasn't banned him yet. He can open most jars on the first try and is only a little afraid of the dark. He still can't load the dishwasher right.

Keep track of Mr. Breakwell's ongoing failings as a father and a human being at ExplodingUnicorn.com or on Facebook at www.Facebook.com/ExplodingUnicorn.

JUST BECAUSE THE UNDEAD'S TASTE BUDS ARE ATROPHYING DOESN'T MEAN YOURS HAVE TO!

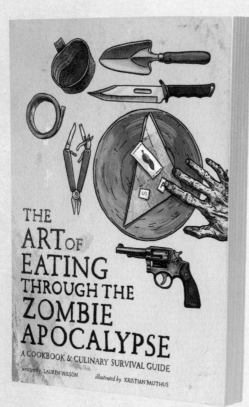

The Art of Eating through the Zombie Apocalypse is a cookbook and culinary field guide for the busy zpoc survivor. With more than 60 recipes (from *Overnight of the Living Dead French Toast* and *It's Not Easy Growing Greens Salad* to *Down & Out Sauerkraut, Honey & Blackberry Mead,* and *Twinkie Trifle*), scads of gastronomic survival tips, and dozens of diagrams and illustrations that help you scavenge, forage, and improvise your way to an artful post-apocalypse meal, *The Art of Eating* is the ideal handbook for efficient food sourcing and inventive meal preparation in the event of an undead uprising.